CRIME
Mapping

D0850997

STUDIES IN CRIME & PUNISHMENT

David A. Schultz and Christina DeJong
General Editors

Vol. 8

PETER LANG
New York • Washington, D.C./Baltimore • Bern
Frankfurt am Main • Berlin • Brussels • Vienna • Oxford

Irvin B. Vann and G. David Garson

CRIME
Mapping

New Tools for Law Enforcement

PETER LANG
New York • Washington, D.C./Baltimore • Bern
Frankfurt am Main • Berlin • Brussels • Vienna • Oxford

Library of Congress Cataloging-in-Publication Data

Vann, Irvin B.
Crime mapping: new tools for law enforcement / Irvin B. Vann and G. David Garson.
p. cm. — (Studies in crime and punishment; vol. 8)
Includes bibliographical references.
1. Crime analysis—United States—Data processing. 2. Crime prevention—United
States—Data processing. 3. Information storage and retrieval systems—Criminal
investigation—United States. 4. Geographic information systems—United States.
5. Digital mapping—United States. I. Vann, Irvin B. II. Title.
III. Studies in crime and punishment; v. 8.
HV7936.C88G37   363.25—dc21   2003002789
ISBN 0-8204-5785-X
ISSN 1529-2444

Bibliographic information published by **Die Deutsche Bibliothek**.
Die Deutsche Bibliothek lists this publication in the "Deutsche
Nationalbibliografie"; detailed bibliographic data is available
on the Internet at http://dnb.ddb.de/.

Cover design by Dutton & Sherman Design

The paper in this book meets the guidelines for permanence and durability
of the Committee on Production Guidelines for Book Longevity
of the Council of Library Resources.

Contents

Figures

Acknowledgments

The authors want to acknowledge Dr. Rachael Bobba of the Police Foundation's Crime Mapping Laboratory and Mr. Matthew Perry of the Charlotte–Mecklenburg Police Department for generously providing maps actually used in police operations. We also want to acknowledge Mr. James Klopovic of the North Carolina Governor's Crime Commission for his willingness to read and make suggestions for improving many parts of the written manuscript.

Irvin B Vann and G. David Garson

Introduction

Everyone has seen an old police drama with detectives and police chiefs intently staring at a large, wall-mounted map with multicolored pins to indicate crime locations. French cartographers in the nineteenth century were among the first to map crime locations in an attempt to look for nation-wide patterns. In the United States the use of "pin mapping" has been traced back to before 1900 by the New York City Police Department. Although these types of maps were important tools for fighting crime in the twentieth century, actual pin maps had several shortcomings addressed by the development of computerized geographic information systems (GIS). Geographic information systems are a collection of technologies designed to interactively query, analyze, and visually display spatial data. The traditional wall map was a static entity lacking the capability to answer queries, or to rearrange data into new relationships, or to be archived for later reference. All these operations were made possible through the basic functions of a GIS system.

The transition from paper to computerized crime mapping began slowly in late 1970s as the largest and most innovative police departments began using mainframe computers and specially trained personnel to create maps. The spread of computerized crime mapping continued at a slow pace until the 1990s, when computers with the necessary memory, speed, and computational power became generally affordable to both police departments and the public at large. The results of the 1999 nationwide survey conducted by the Crime Mapping Research Center indicated that large departments of more than 100 sworn officers continued to be the predominant users of computerized crime mapping. Computerized crime mapping is rapidly becoming an indispensable analysis tool with multiple applications. These applications range from simple pin maps to the more complex challenge of forecasting the movement of crime patterns.

CHAPTER 1

Geographic Information Systems

What Are Geographic Information Systems?

Geographic information systems (GISs) consist of a constellation of hardware and software that integrate computer graphics with a relational database for the purpose of managing and displaying data about geographic locations. These systems link spatial data, graphical presentation, and database management systems in one software "package." Crime mapping is the application of GIS to the management and criminological issues of law enforcement.

Geographic information systems were originally developed as a tool for the natural resource and land management community to monitor variables about forests, wildlife, and other factors affecting ecological systems. In 1963 Roger Tomlinson led the development of the first GIS, the Canada Geographic Information System, to analyze Canada's national land inventory. The needs of this community initially spurred both the development of GIS and many of the analysis operations incorporated in today's popular software packages such as ArcView and MapInfo. As computing migrated from mainframes to personal computers, GIS software followed this migration, expanding its capabilities as both computing power and memory were continuously enhanced.

Computer crime mapping began in the mid 1960s using mainframe computers and punch cards. Since the 1960s, crime mapping has benefited greatly from the general advance of computer technology, allowing for the spread of computerized crime mapping and the ability to experiment easily with various types of cartographic analysis. The latest development in crime mapping is using the Internet to share crime data with citizens by placing various maps on police websites. Many jurisdictions provide information on the location of burglaries, car thefts, and other public disturbance crimes. Using the Internet also provides an opportunity for feedback from citizens regarding police services and an opportunity for police agencies to demonstrate their effectiveness to the community at large.

Geographic Information Systems Components

If a GIS is a constellation of both hardware and software, this constellation is divided into four subsystems: the data input subsystem, a data storage and retrieval system, the manipulation and analysis system, and the reporting subsystem. The data input subsystem consists of the peripheral devices used to create, import, and access data. The data storage and retrieval system consists of on-line and off-line storage devices and media. The manipulation and analysis system has two aspects: the database management system and the geographic or spatial analysis system. The final subsystem is the output subsystem, which allows for the visual representation of the data on a computer screen or a print, most often in the form of maps.

The database management system of a GIS is a relational database that supports queries of records and fields and is especially useful for storing information about spatial data known as attributes. One of the most powerful capabilities of a GIS is the integration of spatial and attribute data. Spatial data describe the location of something while attribute data provide more information about the spatial event. For example, spatial data about a crime incident include *where* the event happened while the attribute data may include all of the other data about the crime collected by a law enforcement agency and stored in its record management system.

There are four important functions of the DBMS used in a GIS for stored data: sorting, reordering, subsetting, and searching. For example, a database of crimes may be sorted by type to view cases in ascending or descending order of severity. The same database of crimes may be reordered by some other attribute such as zip code or police zone to display the types of crime committed in a particular area. Creating subsets of the data involves using the "query language" of the GIS or some other software package. In creating a subset of the data, one creates new data based on a set of criteria, for example, a new data set of the crimes of a particular type. Finally, it may be more important to search for a *particular* crime of interest as opposed to more generalized searching for crimes with given traits.

The spatial information manipulated by a GIS is found in two formats known as vector and raster. Understanding the difference between the types is important in selecting the appropriate data for crime mapping and analysis. In comparing data structures to music, Clarke (1997) used a famous analogy to describe raster data as being similar to the music of Mozart and vector data as being similar to Beethoven. Mozart's music is said to be detailed, repetitive, and highly structured. Raster information is similar in characteristics being structured of uniform cells or grids. The cells or grids are assigned only one value each and are arrayed like a checkerboard. In contrast to raster data, vector data are similar to the music of Beethoven, rapid and efficient with little repetition.

Examples of raster data are aerial photographs, scanned images, and grid-based data. Satellite and other remote sensing products that are discussed later in this book are common examples of grid-based data. If you look at a raster image under a magnifying glass, you will see that it is ultimately composed of points. When an image such as an aerial photograph is enlarged, the points are drawn further apart, and the image becomes grainy or jagged.

In vector images the building blocks are X, Y points known as nodes, and directions on how to draw lines to other nodes. When a vector map is enlarged, the lines are just drawn further apart, and the image will not deteriorate like the raster image. Also, less memory space is required for storing vector data. Raster data such as a standard aerial photograph may take as much as 100 megabytes of storage for just one image. By contrast, vector data for an entire county road system may take less than 10. For this reason, most maps in GIS are vector graphics.

Spatial Analysis with GIS

The spatial analysis system of a GIS implements five types of general functions:

- Buffering
- Nearest-neighbor search
- Overlay operations
- Connectivity analysis
- Network analysis

Buffering operations are used extensively in crime mapping in conjunction with creating pin maps. A buffer is a circle or polygon drawn around a location such as a school or a public building. An example of buffering operations is using a GIS to draw a 1,000-foot drug-free zone around a school or playground. Another example is to buffer an intersection or address to determine the number of ex-offenders living in an area.

Nearest-neighbor search identifies objects that are in closest proximity to an object of interest using spatial or other attributes. For example, this function may be used to find the addresses of previous offenders who live closest to a criminal incident such as a convenience store robbery. The additional search attribute may be for offenders with a prior history of robbing convenience stores.

Overlay operations involve placing various layers of information on top of each other, creating new relationships from the existing data. This type of operation is one of the basic strengths of a GIS. Overlay operations allow the crime analyst to look at how particular crimes intersect with other interesting variables such as police beat, school zones, neighborhood boundaries, economic variables, and the like.

Connectivity analysis identifies areas connected to other areas and is used in conjunction with contiguity analysis to identify areas with common boundaries. Presently, connectivity analysis is used to modify and realign police districts and patrol areas as part of resource allocation. Using special software, realignment is accomplished by affiliating different polygon areas to create new alignments among established districts.

Network analysis involves spatial calculations to determine the shortest distances, fastest routes, or appropriate service areas by street. Using network analysis, emergency services can calculate the fastest routes to a crime or fire, sending directions in real time straight to emergency vehicles. Network analysis can also be used to identify optional locations for police stations or to determine which street ranges should be assigned to which precincts (districting problems). Finally, network analysis can be used for routine law enforcement tasks such as establishing police beats based on crime incidents or establishing delivery routes for supply vehicles.

Building Spatial Databases
for Crime Analysis

When an 89-year-old woman was murdered in Pasadena, California, police were forced to spend hundreds of hours sifting through stacks and stacks of small pawn ticket slips in order to find items stolen in the course of the crime. Pawnshop transactions are only one example of information that, if incorporated in an electronic database, has the potential to greatly assist in the timely solution of crimes. Minneapolis's Automated Pawn System, for instance, increased hits on stolen property by 300% in its first year of operation (McKay 2001). When that database also contains spatial information on pawnshop and customer locations, then it becomes possible to track pawnshop stolen property hits visually over time and to overlay these crime trends on maps tracking thefts and burglaries, distribution of law enforcement resources, and other useful information. Such use of crime mapping has been a routine part of law enforcement in many jurisdictions for some time (Maltz, Gordon, and Friedman 1991; Block, Dabdoub, and Fregly 1995; MacAlister 1996; Weisburd and McEwan 1997; Velasco and Boba 2000a).

There are several reasons for taking a spatial view of crime, which necessitates the building of spatial databases. Crime is spatially concentrated by neighborhood. The structure of metropolitan areas is related to violent crime (Block 1979; Blau and Blau 1982). Assigning patrol personnel and other law enforcement resources must be done on a spatial basis because crime has a spatial basis (Fyfe 1991). Furthermore, new, more effective strategies of "community policing" emphasize the importance of neighborhood (spatial) variables such as employment, business structure, educational resources, bars, culture, and other conditioners of crime (Brantingham and Brantingham 1975; Roncek and Bell 1981; Bursik and Webb 1982; Cooke 1993; Crime Mapping Laboratory 2000a). Data on many of these conditioners are already collected by the U.S. Census and need only to be linked to a law enforcement jurisdiction's crime mapping operations (Brassel and Utano 1979). Indeed, population density and population change in a given area are both conditioners of crime (Choldin and Roncek 1976; Jackson 1984). Finally, because criminal activity displays interjurisdictional mobility, spatial databases are important in tracking the movement of crime across law enforcement boundaries (Deutsch 1984).

A spatial approach to crime analysis is part of a problem-oriented strategy for policing, as opposed to a reactive strategy (see Goldstein 1979, 1990). Deborah Osborne, a crime analyst for the Buffalo (NY) Police Department, put it this way:

> Despite the reality that police cannot and are not responsible to address the root causes of crime, it is true that policing strategies have been known to reduce crime, not just displace it. The traditional reactive policing that is based in responses to calls for service is not the only type of policing in existence. Problem oriented policing, which looks to assess the other, non-policing issues that may be involved in some crime areas/situations, if implemented in reality rather than theory, looks for those causes and offers a format to involve stakeholders (not just the police) in arriving at creative and responsible solutions. (Osborne 2001)

Creating the infrastructure to be able to look for creative, responsible solutions is what designing and building a spatial database for crime analysis is all about.

Problem-oriented policing is a proactive approach to crime. As such it assumes a capacity to analyze data to identify problems and their causes as a basis for developing countermeasures and interventions to attack crime. Eck and Spelman (1988) described the analysis needed for problem-oriented policing under the acronym SARA, standing for scanning, analysis, response, and assessment. While these four stages of analysis are more general than GIS or even computing, crime mapping has emerged as a preeminent support tool for problem-oriented policing (LaVigne,

1999). For "scanning," crime maps quickly identify crime clusters and hot spots, both in general and by criteria such as time of day, type of crime, or location in a time series. For "analysis," crime maps draw on complex relational databases that let analysts relate crime to almost any variable imaginable, such as street lighting, school zones, transportation arteries, land use category, or location of liquor stores. For "response," crime maps can be used strategically (e.g., redrawing police precinct lines to more effectively conform to crime patterns) and tactically (e.g., extrapolating serial crimes to predict anticipated targets, using spatiotemporal analysis as discussed later). Finally, for "assessment," the last stage of the SARA model of problem-oriented policing, crime maps provide "before" and "after" overviews depicting the effect of a law enforcement intervention that can show if there are ancillary effects, such as displacement of crime to neighborhoods outside the intervention area.

Data for crime analysis can come from a wide variety of sources: police departments themselves, of course, for calls for service, arrests, traffic accidents, citations, suspect databases, sex offender information, and more; base maps of the city, usually from city planning or tax departments; bus stop locations from the transportation department; school location and building layouts from the school board; alarm locations from the fire department; lighting information from the electric utility; aerial photographs from regional agencies; demographic data from the U.S. Census; other data purchased from commercial data vendors; and so on.

An illustration of a database system is the Automated Tactical Analysis of Crime (ATAC), used by the Tempe (AZ) Police Department in conjunction with a GIS (Bair 2000). The database system starts with an "Entry Module, " which allows an easy, error-checked way to enter crime data. The "Hub" or "Matrix" is where the data are housed and displayed and where one can select and sort crime incidents. The "Query Wizard" lets analysts do complex searches by word part, word, phrase, or soundex (sounds like) criteria.

The "Structured Query Language Viewer (SQL)" allows users to view query results, edit them, and copy them. "SQL Builder" is the part of the database that lets users create, edit, or issue SQL database commands. The "Trend Wizard" component of the database lets analysts weight crime incident traits by importance (e.g., suspect description would be weighed more for robbery than for burglary),[1] after which an incident can be compared with all other incidents to find similar ones. The "Trend Wizard" can also compare all incidents with each other in order to uncover clusters of similar crimes. The "Time Series Module" lets analysts implement one of several statistical models, such as day of the week analysis to understand, say, how Friday crime differs from Sunday crime. Results may be displayed in tables and graphs or can be input into a GIS like ArcView or MapInfo (the two most popular in police work) to be mapped.

A second example of building a spatial database to fight crime is the Community Safety Information System (CSIS) developed by the Winston-Salem (NC) Police Department (American City & County Staff 2000). The Community Safety Information System allows city law enforcement officials, city administrators, and others to view trends in juvenile delinquency using crime maps. Developed under the Strategic Approaches to Community Safety Initiative of the U.S. Department of Justice, CSIS is based on data from the police department, sheriff's department, school system, social services, and probation office. Additional map layers are available to show census information, locations of abandoned houses, alcohol-related establishments, schools, and more. The password-protected spatial database can be accessed on the Internet using form-based queries, yielding maps sent to the user's own computer. The Community Safety Information System allowed Winston-Salem police (and civil leaders) to pinpoint "hotspot" areas such as certain convenience stores, dead-end streets, and other locations where offenses were clustered. Policy results included planning for after-school and mentoring programs as well as law enforcement officials clean-up operations. Maps also helped clarify crime problems and secure the involvement of clergy, social workers, probation officers, and others as part of a genuine community policing approach to juvenile crime.

Crime databases and dissemination of maps and information drawn from them have many advantages for the police and for the community. Increasingly, maps and information are disseminated via the Internet. For instance, the San Diego Police Department pioneered putting crime maps on the Internet back in 1996, developing a multi-agency, interactive website in 1999, which allowed access to information on crimes, crime surveys, arrests, traffic incidents, and more, with users able to search by city, police beat, neighborhood, or even street as well as by incident type, time of day, and day of week (Wartell 2001).

Internet-based crime information dissemination leads to lower staff work processing inquiries, more community awareness and involvement in community policing, more citizen anti-victimization efforts, and greater interagency data sharing (e.g., among social welfare, public works, public housing, schools, hospitals, parks and recreation departments, and urban planning and other divisions). Public data dissemination also is a means to data verification as public scrutiny brings discrepancies to light, in some cases discouraging internal law enforcement agency efforts to manipulate data "to look better."

Geographic information systems allow policy-makers to examine variables that are otherwise hidden from view in conventional databases and reports. For instance, the Department of Housing and Urban Development used GIS to investigate whether crime within public housing projects was more prevalent than crime in other areas (Hyatt 1999). Public opinion associates crime with public housing projects, but in fact crime statistics supporting (or refuting) this belief have been largely unavailable for the simple reason that conventional police databases reported crimes for precincts and other large reporting districts covering large geographic areas much more extensive than housing projects themselves. Using GIS, however, it was possible to map crimes within 50-meter, 100-meter, 250-meter buffers around each housing project in sampled cities and to compare crime rates with those in areas of similar size in otherwise comparable city zones not having housing projects and thus answer policy questions about crime in public housing.

The construction of databases for crime mapping has fallen largely to local communities, though there are now some regional efforts (discussed in a later section). At the national level, the National Archive of Criminal Justice Data (NACJD) operates under the aegis of the Inter-University Consortium for Political and Social Research at the University of Michigan. The NACJD archives criminal justice databases for research and education, drawing on data from the Bureau of Justice Statistics, the National Institute of Justice, the Office of Juvenile Justice and Delinquency Prevention, and others. However, at this time few NACJD data sets have spatial fields needed for crime mapping. Also at the federal level, and specializing in data sets with spatial fields, is the National Spatial Data Infrastructure, representing some seventeen federal agencies as well as state-level GIS councils and others, but as of 2003 it housed no criminal justice data.

Promoting GIS Crime Databases

The Crime Mapping Research Center (CMRC) was founded in 1997 as part of the National Institute of Justice within the U.S. Department of Justice. The mission of the CMRC is to promote the use of crime mapping in America's law enforcement departments and agencies, of which only 13% then used GIS (Elber 2001: 19). The CMRC offers free software such as CrimeStat (spatial statistical tools) and also provides grants for software development (e.g., Crime Analysis Extension for ArcView was the result of a CMRC grant). The CMRC also develops distance learning tools for the law enforcement community, such as CrimeMap Tutorial, a computer program for self-paced learning of skills needed to produce crime maps using either of the two leading GIS packages used by police departments, ArcView and Map-Info.[2] Other branches of the Department of Justice also promote crime mapping. The DOJ Criminal Division, for instance, distributes SCAS and RCAGIS software for ArcView to map crime incidents.[3] Likewise, the National Institute of Justice's National Law Enforcement and Corrections Technology Center in Denver provides free courses on the use of crime mapping software. Other free courses are available from the Police Foundation's Crime Mapping Laboratory, based on funding from the Department of Justice's community-oriented policing services (COPS) office. The COPS office has also funded purchase of GIS equipment by police departments under its making officer redeployment effective (MORE) grant program and other grants are available through the BJA.[4] Finally, COPS provides a guide to a wide variety of software relevant to crime mapping (Crime Mapping Laboratory 2001).

Crime Databases and Public Access

The purpose of creating a crime database is to disseminate information more effectively, including to members of the public and their elected representatives. Interactive Internet access to constantly updated crime trend information is the emerging norm for law enforcement agencies.[5] For instance, the Illinois State Police illustrates a state-level law enforcement agency that began offering crime, registered sex offender, and traffic maps via the web starting in 1999. By 2000, citizens could view photographs of registered sex offenders, as well as name, address, date of birth, and type of offense (either child or adult offender). Likewise the Illinois State Police makes fatal car crash information available by level of geography, date, and crash causes.[6] Where individual Illinois citizens rarely viewed Uniform Crime Reports containing these same data, on-line delivery of data created genuine mass access for citizens. By providing a structured query system with selected information automatically returned without access to raw data, families' privacy is protected. For instance, a query might return information on

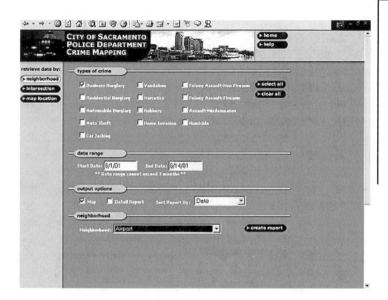

FIGURE 1.1 Sacramento Police Department Internet Access Interface.

whether an accident involved a teen driver, but it would not return any driver names or addresses. An example at the municipal level is the Cambridge (MA) Police Department.[7]

Cambridge is thought to be the first city police department to provide crime pattern and trend data to citizens via the Internet. Though not interactively manipulatable by citizen users, the Cambridge Police Department site provides reviews of most patterns, series, hotspots, and trends identified by its crime analysts. It also provides stories of notable crimes and arrests and covers five of the city's most serious target crimes of the past week except where publication would interfere with ongoing investigations. All statistics and maps are accompanied by written qualitative analyses in an effort to minimize misinterpretation of the data by the public and the press. Another municipal example is the Redlands (CA) Police Department, which uses CrimeView Internet software from the Omega Group to provide crime mapping services and output to users throughout the city, without having to install GIS at separate locations (Schulman

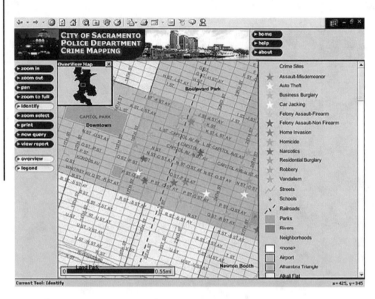

FIGURE 1.2 Sacramento Police Department Internet Output.

2001). An additional example is the system of the Sacramento (CA) Police Department, shown in Figures 1.1 and 1.2.

A more advanced example of Internet-based access to crime data is the "Crime Viewer" supplied via the Internet by the Austin Police Department (APD). Internet users may choose to see data aggregated by police patrol area, zip codes, census tracts, or neighborhoods (Johnson 2001). Users can input an address and see crime within 500 feet of the address. A rectangle can be dragged anywhere on the map to get a summary of crime within that rectangle. An "Identify" function lets users click on the map to see information about police districts, neighborhood APD representatives, and census tract or zip code information. The APD system not only provides citizens with more useful and more immediate information, it also frees crime analysts to conduct actual analyses of crime patterns without the need to respond to as many citizen information requests.[8]

Misinterpretation is a major issue in crime mapping because of the technical and geostatistical elements involved. A prime example has to do with geocoding rates.[9] The geocoding rate for a given map is the percent of addresses that are accurately matched. Lincoln (NE) Chief of Police Tom Casady noted, "Last year, police officers in Lincoln, Nebraska, responded to 140,000 dispatches. If the source data were 100% accurate, and dispatch records were geocoded accurately 99% of the time, 1,400 dots would be misplaced on [or missing from] the resulting map" (Casady 1999: 2). In practice, actual geocoding rates are often well below 99%. One solution when providing crime-mapping data is to display the geocoding rate along with each map. However, will citizens understand a phrase such as "geocoding rate = 82%"? If not, should the agency provide a statement such as "Geocoding rates of 80%–90% provide accuracy suitable for discerning broad spatial trends in crime but should not be construed to be accurate at the block level"? Should an even-longer and more detailed statement of qualification be made? Ultimately the crime mapper fantasizes about enrolling citizens in a short course on geographic information systems before allowing them to view and interpret crime maps on their own.[10] Fear of public misinterpretation of crime maps remains a serious impediment to fuller public access.

In law enforcement, the establishment of access to crime-mapping information entails numerous policy decisions about access. Should data on juvenile crimes be available? Should data on sex crimes be available? Should data on citizen complaints be available, or only on arrests? How closely should crimes be pinpointed: neighborhood, street, 100-block, or actual address? Should crime data be available by school, housing project, alcohol-serving establishment, or other entities, even though these entities may not themselves be direct progenitors of crime? What disclaimers should the law enforcement agency give on the currency or validity of data that are released? How much supplementary interpretation and commentary should agencies provide along with raw data displays?[11]

Some standards are emerging in answer to these questions. For instance, on the matter of level of aggregation of crime data, negative reactions have been observed when data are aggregated to the neighborhood level because map shading of an entire neighborhood as high in crime may distort the true picture, which might be that there is a strong problem in a few given blocks but not throughout an entire neighborhood. Neighbors in the safe blocks resent being portrayed just the same as the "problem blocks," and such portrayal may affect where people buy homes or may even affect insurance, loans, and property values. At the same time, pinpointing crimes to the actual address violates individual privacy and raises fears of re-victimization. Therefore an emerging standard is to map crime to the 100-block level, avoiding identification of specific addresses but also avoiding stereotyping entire neighborhoods.

In terms of access to sex offender information, in many cases policy decisions have been made by state legislatures or even Congress. After the passage in 1996 at the federal level of Megan's Law (P.L. 104–145), the publication of sex offender registries became mandatory and in most jurisdictions was implemented in electronic form, though not always on the Internet (some require citizens to view sex offender data on a computer located in a police department, for instance). Thus, since 1998 Virginia has listed on the Internet the names, ages, home addresses, conviction records, and photographs of sex offenders, receiving over 650,000 website hits in its first two months alone.[12] Another example is Pierce County, Washington, where the Sheriff's Department website[13] houses a database of all registered sex and kidnapping offenders within the jurisdiction. Website visitors can obtain not only general information about sex offenders but also can enter an address to obtain an interactive map that displays all registered sex offenders residing within a 0.5-mile radius of the address, and then visitors can obtain the names of these offenders and related offense information.

Over the protests of civil libertarians, privacy rights accorded others are routinely denied to sex offenders. In addition to name and address information, it is not unusual for registries to make personal descriptions and even photographs available. Needless to say, the denial of privacy to sex offenders raises serious issues about inaccuracies in the data. Agencies post disclaimers of liabilities but civil libertarians argue that current practices amount to double punishment and that sex offense data should only be presented on a 100-block or higher level of aggregation, hiding individual-level information, like other crime data.

The era of Internet access to data has brought actual or potential mass citizen access to data that, while available through traditional, manual archive-hunting, was for all practical purposes protected by the burdensome barriers to retrieving it. This came to the fore in the Supreme Court case, *U.S. Department of Justice v. Reporters Committee* (489 U.S. 749, 1989), where the Court upheld the privacy interest of citizens in the "practical obscurity" of paper records (Hammitt 2000). This decision of the Supreme Court seems to open the door for agencies to create a dual standard, allowing public access to hard-to-retrieve paper records in file cabinets while denying public access to the same information in easily accessible electronic form! Most court rulings, however, have applied the same standards to electronic and paper formatted data (Reporters Committee for Freedom of the Press 1998).

Federal Resources for Crime Mapping

The number of agencies that use and provide GIS resources has mushroomed in the past two decades. In fact it has been estimated that 85% of all government agencies use GIS in one way or another, serving a burgeoning community of GIS end users. A number of federal resources have emerged as centers of training, support, and technical services. The federal government has supported computerized crime mapping through many governmental and nongovernmental agencies, but the primary agency supporting computerized crime mapping is the Department of Justice. In fiscal year 2001 the federal government provided an estimated $81 million in various grants to spread the use of information technologies among police agencies.

The Department of Justice, through its research arm, the National Institute of Justice, has encouraged application of computerized crime mapping to police functions since the mid 1980s. In 1986 the National Institute of Justice funded a study in Chicago both to implement and to assess the impact of a map-based crime analysis system. Following this initial research, the National Institute of Justice funded another study in 1989 to assess whether crime mapping could be used effectively to combat street-level drug markets. The effectiveness of crime mapping in these studies in conjunction with the increasing availability of GIS encouraged larger police departments to adopt computerized crime mapping as a crime analysis tool in the 1990s. A 1999 survey by the Crime Mapping Research Center indicated that 36% of the departments with more than 100 officers are now using computerized crime mapping.

In 1999 the Department of Justice issued a report entitled *Mapping Out Crime*. The report outlined support for using GIS and crime mapping to drive management decisions as well as to encourage crime prevention partnerships between law enforcement agencies and local communities. *Mapping Out Crime* proposed a vision for law enforcement that included a technology-based method of delivering police services. This data-driven aspect of policing included the use of current information analyzed with advanced mapping and analytic techniques.

Department of Justice

The Department of Justice is the Cabinet level agency responsible for law and justice operations in the United States. As part of its mission, the DOJ funds criminal justice research through its various subordinate agencies. Funding for crime mapping falls into three broad categories: research on

using crime mapping in law enforcement, funding for software and hardware, and training for crime analysts to use
various GIS tools. The Department of Justice administers its
crime-mapping efforts through its subordinate agencies.
These agencies include the National Institute of Justice, the
Crime Mapping Research Center, and the Crime Mapping
and Analysis Program.

The National Institute of Justice is the research and development agency of the U.S. Department of Justice and is the
only federal agency solely dedicated to researching crime
control and justice issues. The National Institute of Justice
has focused on using the social and physical sciences in its
efforts to reduce crime, improve administration, and promote public safety.

In February 1997 the National Institute of Justice established the CMRC, which became the federal government's
clearinghouse for computerized crime mapping. The
center's goals are to promote research, evaluation, development, and dissemination of GIS technologies for crime
analysis and criminal justice research. During this book's
writing the CMRC became the Mapping and Analysis for
Public Safety (MAPS) office, still under the National Institute of Justice. To achieve its goals the center's mission
statement outlines four functions: research, evaluation, development, and dissemination. The research activities of
MAPS include fellowships for university academics and
skilled practitioners to work independently on computerized crime-mapping topics.

To disseminate its research efforts the center conducts an
annual international conference, and the staff makes pres-
entations at various forums throughout the United States
and abroad. Other major dissemination efforts include the
center's website at http://www.ojp.usdoj.gov/nij/maps/. The
website serves as the clearinghouse of the center and a
starting point to learn about crime mapping as well as connecting with other members of the crime-mapping community. The MAPS office also operates an Internet listserv for

members to share information or ask questions regarding crime analysis and computerized crime mapping.

As part of the growing interest in the field of computerized crime mapping, the Crime Mapping Research Center published its first solicitation in 2001 to fund research through a granting process. The center administered approximately $300,000 as part of its goals to promote research, evaluation, development, and dissemination of GIS technologies as well as the spatial analysis of crime.

The Crime Mapping and Analysis Program (CMAP) is a program of the National Law Enforcement and Corrections Technology Center, a component of the National Institute of Justices Office of Science and Technology, and provides assistance to law enforcement agencies in applying technology to justice and policing. In the area of GIS for law enforcement the CMAP is responsible for providing assistance in the area of crime intelligence analysis as well as computerized crime mapping. The CMAP program also provides assistance in the areas of global positioning systems, automatic vehicle location systems, and electronic home monitoring of community corrections clientele.

Housing and Urban Development

The U.S. Department of Housing and Urban Development (HUD) is another federal agency developing expertise in the area of computerized crime mapping. HUD is the agency responsible for administering the more than 14,000 public housing developments in the United States. In 1999 HUD published a study entitled *Guidebook for Measuring Crime in Public Housing with Geographic Information Systems,* seeking to facilitate the systematic tracking of crime in public housing communities.

One of the many aspects of housing administration is differentiating the levels and types of crime in public housing from their surroundings. Unfortunately, many police departments measure crime in larger geographic areas normally described as "zones," "beats," or "patrol areas." This method of measuring crime usually incorporates the public housing area into the greater area, lessening the ability to study crime specifically in public housing.

The *Guidebook* proposes that both police departments and public housing authorities should form a mutually beneficial data partnership in the mapping of crime in public housing. These data partnerships can serve a two-fold purpose: to enhance the ability to measure crime in public housing and to aid community-oriented policing efforts in the same areas. Further research suggested that public housing area maps helped local police departments adjust their routine patrols to include public housing properties, providing public housing residents' better access to emergency services (Hyatt 1999).

Other Institutions

The federal government also supports crime-mapping research and implementation by using outside agencies through the grant-funding process. Outside agencies receiving grants may be state entities or nongovernmental organizations. Two prominent nongovernmental agencies providing support for the federal government's efforts in crime mapping are the Institute for Law and Justice (ILJ) and the Police Foundation.

The Institute for Law and Justice is a private corporation that focuses its efforts on the various aspects of training, evaluation, and research in the criminal justice community and frequently receives grants from the Department of Justice and its subordinate agencies and has extensively published in the area of law enforcement, victimization, and science and technology. Many of its publications are freely available for downloading at http://www.ilj.org/publications.html. For instance, one of the institute's recent contributions to computerized crime-mapping literature is a timely report entitled *Mapping and Data Confidentiality*. This particular report addresses issues associated with sharing crime-mapping data within the contexts of interagency cooperation, formal research, and public service.

The Police Foundation was founded in 1970 through the

auspices of the Ford Foundation as a nonpartisan, non-profit, and independent foundation with an overall mission to improve police practices. The foundation's Crime Mapping Laboratory was initially established with the assistance of the Office of Community Oriented Policing Services of the Department of Justice. The purpose of the Crime Mapping Laboratory is to provide assistance and information to police departments along with developing the physical and theoretical infrastructure to further innovations in police and criminological theory. The foundation maintains a website at http://www.policefoundation.org/ with a link to its Crime Mapping Laboratory. The Crime Mapping Laboratory also publishes the *Crime Mapping News,* which is available for downloading in the Adobe Acrobat (pdf) format from its website.

Summary

For the past 10 years using geographic information systems has enhanced crime mapping and analysis and is now a routine function of law enforcement. Computer-generated maps on a projection screen have replaced the detectives intently staring at a pin-filled map on a wall. The importance of GIS in crime analysis has been recognized at the national level by the Department of Justice. To support research and development of computerized crime analysis, the federal government directly provides its own resources to the field as well as working with foundations and non-profit agencies. The Police Foundation is one agency outside of the federal government that supports research in the area of computerized crime mapping. Within its research division, the Department of Justice established the Crime Mapping Research Center as a central clearinghouse for crime mapping. Recently the center was renamed the Mapping Analysis for Public Safety (MAPS) office. To use a GIS for crime analysis, the integration of various types information becomes an important issue. Jurisdictions must have access to a variety of information to create maps from crime data.

Questions

1. What is a geographic information system (GIS)?
2. Identify and describe the five types of general functions common to GIS spatial analysis.
3. Why would a police department want to create a spatial database?
4. What organization in the Department of Justice serves as the clearinghouse for crime mapping? What are its four objectives?
5. What are some positive issues with making crime data easily accessible to the public?
6. From a police department level, describe some negative issues with making crime data easily accessible to the public.

CHAPTER 2

Crime-Mapping Basics

Pin Mapping of Crime Locations: What Is Pin Mapping?

Automated pin maps for crime analysis are created in a GIS system when a street centerline data layer is displayed in conjunction with crime data. Crime data are usually entered automatically as a batch into the GIS from computerized call-for-service data or from records management systems. Additionally, most GIS software packages have an option whereby the technician or even the patrol officer can enter addresses into the system manually. Once the data are entered, the GIS then "matches" the crime addresses to the street centerline data and displays the results in a visual

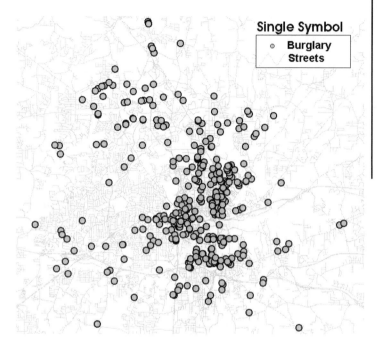

Single Symbol

○ **Burglary**
   Streets

FIGURE 2.1 Burglary Pin Map. *Crime Mapping Laboratory, Police Foundation, 2002.*

format that becomes a map. Creating pin maps is the GIS function most frequently reported by users of computerized crime maps.

One of the shortcomings of automated pin mapping is that the locations of crimes as they are displayed on the map are approximate and not exact. When addresses are matched in a process known as geocoding, the position of the address is interpolated. For example, if the address of a crime occurred at 123 Main Street, the GIS may find the 100 section of the street and then "guess" where 23 is located. In the best possible scenario, the street name entered into the GIS will be found in the attributes of the centerline data and spelled correctly, resulting in a "hit." Failure to identify a location for 123 Main Street is considered a "miss." The major software packages such as ArcView and MapInfo provide qualitative feedback on batch geocoding in the form of a hit rate. The hit rate is simply the ratio of "hits" to "misses" in the geocoding process.

The lack of a "hit" usually requires the technician or analyst to enter the data manually or to attempt to "clean" the data before they are reentered. In cleaning data the analyst is usually looking for some of these common mistakes in recording address data: misspelling the street name, providing an incorrect suffix or directional indicator, or recording an out-of-range address. Although there is no formal minimum for hit rates, the rule of thumb is that anything less than 60% may lead an analyst to make false assumptions regarding a crime trend. Few crime maps have a 100% hit rate or may be said to be 100% accurate.

On the Crime Mapping Research Center's electronic discussion list a considerable number of the technical questions addressed to members discuss various methods for successfully cleaning address data. This is understandable since a major city may have hundreds of incidents input from various sources that require mapping in the course of a week. Cleaning the data becomes important to providing timely intelligence for patrol officers.

Displaying Particular Crimes and Places

Once a set of incidents is cleaned and an acceptable number of hits are displayed, the next step is to use a database management systems (DBMS) function known as "selection by attribute" to display specific types of crimes rather than a confusing sea of points. A very basic DBMS function is to select particular crimes and to visually display them in different colors by type of crime just as in the old days of wall maps. However, this still leaves the issue of easily picking out an item of interest on a busy screen display or map. One simple solution is to use a different-shaped point for a particular class of crime. Responding to customer demand for specialized displays, the creators of both MapInfo and the ESRI products have included special symbol sets for criminal activity in their respective software packages. It is much easier and more eye-catching to pick out a unique symbol, such as a pistol for an assault, than to scan for dot of a particular colored or plain geometric shape.

To further reduce the clutter on the map, an analyst may want to display only one particular type of crime from a set of incidents. Using the "attribute selection" function of a DBMS, an analyst can select for a particular category of crime like burglary. After an initial selection, if an analyst thinks there are smaller patterns contained in the bigger one, the DBMS allows the operator to query the data set further in the search for more precise information. For example, within a set of burglaries an analyst may only be interested in burglaries with a certain characteristic or modus operandi (MO) such as residential or commercial burglaries.

Selecting by a particular attribute is also useful for examining the spatial relationship of various attributes of a crime incident. For example, characteristics of either the victim or the offender may be interesting to the analyst. The race, gender, and street address of either victim or offender may help a crime analyst to spot distinct patterns. Some real-life questions may be, "What are the characteristics of robbery victims in or near a local park?" Or "Where do apprehended offenders live, and is there a pattern to their commuting?"

Interesting crime patterns are not limited to victim and offender attributes. The place where an incident happens may also have unique characteristics. For example, what types of commercial establishments are the most frequent targets of burglaries? Where are they located? Do they form an identifiable cluster with a predictable pattern? Are there other unique attributes shared among crime scenes? Some of these dot patterns are unique and numerous enough to form "hot spots," a topic discussed in the next section of this chapter.

A basic GIS analysis function useful in conjunction with a pin map is buffering. By buffering a point, an analyst seeks to establish something interesting regarding the crime within some number of feet. For example, did a drug arrest occur within 1,000 feet of an elementary school? Or is there a paroled sex offender living within 1,000 feet of a "flashing" incident? Of course buffering does not have to be

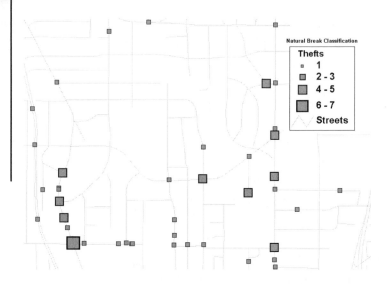

FIGURE 2.2 Graduated Symbols. *Crime Mapping Laboratory, Police Foundation, 2002.*

done in feet. The major GIS software packages allow for buffering in units ranging from inches and centimeters to miles and kilometers.

Until now the discussion of computerized pin mapping has been restricted to one particular incident in one place. What happens when there are multiple incidents of a crime at the same location? For example, what about a series of burglaries in a single apartment complex within a month? Rather than pepper the map with dots, one on top of the other, the major GIS software packages allow users to manipulate the map symbology. One solution to the "many incidents in one place" problem is to adjust the size of the symbols in the visual display in proportion to the number of incidents at that location. Even though the symbols differ in size, GIS operations like buffering are still available to the analyst.

Successful Uses of Pin Mapping

As we have noted, computerized pin mapping is a significant technological improvement compared to the sticking of colored pins into a wall map. However, new technologies will not spread unless they can be successfully applied to real-world problems. In Chapter 6 we discuss the famous Compstat program used by the New York City Police Department. Initiated in 1994, one of the key components of the Compstat program has been the use of computerized maps for the near real-time analysis of crime. In a 1997 press release, Mayor Rudolph Giuliani credited computer pin mapping in conjunction with crime and statistical analysis with contributing to a 43% reduction in overall crime in New York City from 1993 to 1997.

Another useful application of pin mapping is in small-town or rural police departments. An unedited pin map of a city like New York will be swamped with thousands of points, making interpretation difficult and giving rise to the need to go beyond pin mapping. However, in a more rural environment, pin mapping may be adequate for law enforcement to monitor even multiple categories of crime. All GIS software packages give the user the ability to select symbols in various types and colors. In a smaller jurisdiction different colors may be sufficient to follow a crime trend.

Pin mapping sometimes serves successfully as the only type of crime mapping in smaller communities. Boone, for example, located in western North Carolina, is both a university and a tourist town, with approximately 13,000 year-round residents. The most serious incidents are reported to be vandalism, auto accidents, and alcohol-related incidents. Additionally, there are only a limited number of customers or end users for any GIS product. For Boone and similar communities, pin mapping alone is viewed as an adequate tool for crime analysis.

Beyond Pin Mapping

Pin mapping can be the gateway to other crime-mapping functions, in part because the ability to implement good pin maps implies that the jurisdiction has successfully addressed data issues such as base street maps.

A useful variation of pin mapping is the choropleth map. The choropleth map is simply a shaded or thematic map that uses color intensities rather than dots to communicate information. The choropleth map requires census, political, police boundaries, or even arbitrary grids as polygons to be shaded according to crime intensity. Imagine a large city with many crime incidents occurring in one or more neighborhoods. The sheer number of dots in a pin map could cloud any useable information even if graduated dot sizes were used to indicate multiple instances of a crime. By using a choropleth map an analyst can shade regions based on the level of crime. By convention, as the shading of a color gets darker, the number of incidents are rising. This progressive shading is called a "color ramp."

In terms of analysis, choropleth mapping allows one to examine crime in terms of other variables in the attempt to look for patterns. If census tracts are being used, for instance, then crimes committed within the tract may be analyzed in conjunction with demographic or economic variables. For example, a crime like residential burglary may occur more frequently in one census tract rather than another. A combined form, the dot-density choropleth maps, can indicate the correlation of two variables by letting the thematic shading represent, for instance, level of drug use and letting dots represent auto thefts to show the correlation between these two types of crime. Hotspot analysis, discussed next, is as extension of pin and choropleth mapping. As skills and experience increase, analysts may expand from pin mapping to hotspot mapping as a way of getting even more information payoff.

HotSpot Mapping

Humans have a natural tendency to seek patterns in their attempts to understand seemingly random events in the world around them. In the previous section we discussed basic pin mapping as an introductory step to finding patterns in criminal activity. One benefit of pin mapping is that repeated crimes in a particular location may be shown as distinctive clusters. In a frequently referenced study of crime and place in Minneapolis, Minnesota, it was discovered that much of the crime in that city shared the same physical addresses, with over 50% of the crimes committed in 3% of the addresses found in the police calls-for-service records. In crime mapping such clusters of crimes are referred to as hotspots.

Although the term "hotspot" is commonly used in the language of crime analysis, different experts in the field employ subtle differences of definition. Keith Harries (1999), a noted researcher and contributor in the field of geography and crime analysis, observed that there is no widely accepted definition of the hotspot concept and noted that a rigid, absolute definition may even be impossible. Yet the concept of a hotspot is useful nonetheless in fighting crime, and it gives police agencies and communities a starting point to focus their resources, even though each may define a hotspot slightly differently.

In the first steps of identifying crime hotspots there are three aspects to consider: geographic, temporal/seasonal, and cartographic. First one must approach the term from a geographic perspective. From this viewpoint, criminologists and analysts writing in the field of crime mapping refer to hotspots in two different ways. One definition is that a hotspot is a "point" with limited area such as a bar, hotel, intersection, and so on. Another definition describes a hotspot as being somewhat larger in size, such as the extended surroundings of an apartment complex, a city block, or a park. This definition is usually called a "hotspot area." Each of these definitions also has an additional element of mobility, as hotspots may even displace to other locations under certain conditions due to periods of increased enforcement of nuisance laws. For example, police response to criminal activity may cause the hotspot to move if criminals are displaced to other areas in reaction to the enforcement. Crime mapping is important in determining the location of hotspots since not infrequently tactical-level police officers and supervisors misidentify the location of hotspots based on intuition alone.

Tactical crime analysts define a hotspot as a place where an unusual amount of criminal activity is committed by one or more offenders. For example, a street intersection where the police have made multiple arrests for a single type of crime like prostitution would be considered a hotspot. On a pin map, arrests made at the intersection might be represented either as a collection of points or a scaled symbol for multiple incidents. A study by Buerger, Cohn, and Petrosino (1995) contributed a more refined definition of hotspots by adding the following more formal criteria:

1. No hotspot is more than one standard linear street block.
2. No hotspot extends for more than half a block from either side of an intersection.
3. No hotspot is within one standard linear block of another hotspot.

Determining what constitutes a hotspot area is a bit more complex than just identifying points. The true definition of area boundaries remains one of the basic research questions in computerized crime mapping. As a starting point, areas may be defined by artificial political and administrative boundaries such as census tracts, police beats, or city limits, and there are methods for analyzing crime within these boundaries. However, one of the problems with crime is that it often crosses boundaries, requiring new definitions for an area.

Time and season are another aspect of hotspots. Using the previous example, a street intersection with prostitution arrests may be active only during certain hours, making it a temporal hotspot. One possible method to identify temporal hotspots is by viewing criminal activity throughout a 24-hour day, noting when crime intensifies at a certain location. Advances in desktop computer animation technology now allow the chaining of hour-by-hour maps created by a

GIS so that increasing/decreasing activity in an area can be visually identified through animation of maps.

Hotspots may also develop in response to changing seasonal and environmental factors. For example, burglary incidents increase in the summer due to more open windows and outdoor activity. An apartment complex or a neighborhood might suddenly become an active hotspot during a heat wave or over the course of a summer. Similarly, a mall parking lot may erupt with a series of car break-ins, becoming a temporary hotspot during the busy Christmas shopping season.

There is also a cartographic aspect of hotspots arising from the ability of a GIS to change map scale in the display mode by zooming closer or farther away. On a small-scale map of a city, a collection of points may appear to be one dot. As one zooms closer and the scale becomes larger, the dots begin to separate, and a single hotspot becomes several dots spread over a neighborhood. As you zoom in, at a certain scale you come full circle back to the question, "What is the area definition of a hotspot?"

Identifying Hotspots Through Map Analysis

Since identifying a crime hotspot has an element of subjectivity both researchers and crime analysts are concerned with reliably and objectively identifying them. This is a reasonable concern since not all clusters on a crime map are hotspot clusters. Some clusters are unrelated or random collections of criminal activity. In the effort to identify hotspots reliably, researchers and analysts have begun using various spatial statistics techniques in conjunction with computerized crime mapping. Hotspot analysis using crime mapping is classified into five general techniques: visual interpretation, choropleth mapping, grid-cell analysis, point-pattern or cluster analysis, and spatial autocorrelation.

• Visual Interpretation
The most basic method for identifying hotspots is visual analysis. The crime analyst creates a pin map, notices a

distinctive clustering of crime points, and interprets this as a hotspot. As we have noted earlier, this method carries with it a strong element of subjectivity, even with the additional criteria developed by Buerger. Many of the software packages being developed in the crime-mapping field are attempting to remove this element of subjectivity in identifying hotspots.

• Choropleth Mapping
The choropleth map is simply a thematic map that uses color intensities to communicate information rather than dots. The choropleth map requires some type of boundary system to provide context for the data. The boundary systems are usually defined by census, political, and, in some cases, police boundaries. An example of a choropleth map is one that identifies the highest per-capita homicide rate in a state's counties first by calculating the homicide rate per capita and then using intensity shading to identify the hotspots. In interpreting choropleth maps for analysis, it is important to understand the area unit fallacy. An area unit fallacy is when one assumes that all members within the boundary share the same characteristics. In the state counties example, one would create an area unit fallacy if one assumed all cities and communities within the county boundary had the same homicide rate . Just because one area in a choropleth map is shaded a particular color does not mean crime is uniformly distributed throughout the area. This is a problem with using choropleth maps for visual analysis.

• Grid-Cell Analysis
Grid-cell analysis is the basis for many of the spatial statistics packages being used in crime analysis. In its simplest form, grid-cell analysis begins by using uniform-sized grid cells rather than artificial boundaries like census tracts to overlay an area of interest. In this respect it is usually different from the choropleth map that is usually based only on artificial boundaries. Next, any points falling within a

grid or sometimes neighboring a grid cell are aggregated to one cell. In the final stage of the analysis, unusual clusters are identified for further investigation.

• Point-Pattern or Cluster Analysis
Point-pattern analysis involves identifying an arbitrary starting point and employing statistical algorithms to define clusters of points. For example, one spatial statistic used to identify clusters is the Nearest Neighbor Index. This algorithm examines events clustered around a location to determine if the events are attributable to random chance. The index number is a guide indicating to the analyst the possibility of some common factor among the points.[1]

• Spatial Autocorrelation
Spatial autocorrelation is a different type of statistical algorithm designed to establish spatial relationships among clusters of points. It is based on spatial similarities and traits among the points of interest. Positive spatial autocorrelation indicates that similar cases cluster as they are located closer to each other, possibly indicating the presence of a hotspot. Negative autocorrelation indicates the opposite. If like incidents such as burglary or robbery tend to cluster within one area, spatial autocorrelation can be used to flag situations needing additional law enforcement resources and attention.

Mapping Crime Density

You are probably familiar with the term "density" as used in social science terms such as population density. One method of measuring the concept of population density is to divide the number of people by some other number, usually square miles. Crime density may be measured in per-capita numbers such as the number of crimes per 10,000 or even 100,000 people. Another method of measuring crime density is to count the number of crimes occurring within administrative boundaries or uniformly sized grids.

Crime density may be displayed on a map using three different methods. The first is by using a choropleth (shaded) map as discussed in the section on hotspot analysis. By using this method an analyst displays data within the context of some type of boundary. The second method is to display crime density using smaller and more uniform grids found in raster data.[2] Using uniform grids aids the identification of local crime hotspots contained within boundaries, thereby lessening the area fallacy (assuming crime is uniform throughout a larger jurisdiction). The third method is to add contour lines to a density surface map, a method used extensively in crime analysis to visually identify crime hotspots.

Choropleth Mapping

A basic choropleth map uses color intensities rather than dots to communicate information. Choropleth maps are also called thematic maps or shaded maps. Imagine a large city with many crime incidents occurring in one neighborhood or a series of such incidents. The sheer number of dots could cloud any useable information even if you are using graduated dot sizes to indicate multiple instances of a crime. By using a choropleth map an analyst is able to aggregate numerous crimes up to an area level and then shade the areas with darker colors, indicating a higher number of incidents. Choropleth maps reflect appropriate area averages such as crime rates and population densities. Using the data base management system of a GIS, it is possible to store nominal level data about the area like land use or zoning.

In terms of crime-density analysis, choropleth mapping allows one to examine crime in terms of other variables in the attempt to look for patterns. If census tracts are being used as the boundary system, then crimes committed within the tract may be analyzed in conjunction with demographic or economic variables that are available from the Census Bureau. For example, certain crimes like residential burglary may occur more frequently in one census tract rather than another. The tract with the most frequent occur-

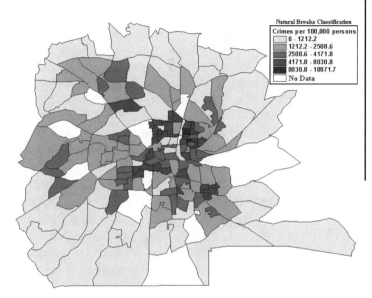

Natural Breaks Classification
Crimes per 100,000 persons
☐ 0 - 1212.2
▨ 1212.2 - 2508.6
▨ 2508.6 - 4171.8
▨ 4171.8 - 8030.8
■ 8030.8 - 18871.7
☐ No Data

FIGURE 2.3 Crime Density Using Graduated Color and Choropleth Mapping. *Crime Mapping Laboratory, Police Foundation, 2002.*

rence may have key economic or demographic characteristics associated with higher crime levels. A tract with frequent burglary might have high-density housing with a transient population, providing many opportunities for offenders.

One disadvantage in using choropleth mapping for crime-density analysis is that political and administrative boundaries are often very irregular in size with shapes constructed for political reasons rather than reasons related to the distribution of crime. Using data aggregation and choropleth mapping, the crime density of one small section of an area may be the single biggest factor influencing the crime-density display. It will appear that an entire area is a crime problem rather than the smaller area within it. Users may conclude the entire area is a problem no matter where the problem is actually located. It then becomes a question of how to focus law enforcement resources. Does an agency choose to try and cover a large area or do they attempt to guess where the smaller crime area is located?

Density Mapping

Recall that in the first chapter two types of data used in GIS were discussed, raster and vector. Using raster data is another way of measuring and visualizing crime density. Raster data can be created by GIS software, which generates a uniform grid of cells to lay over a map or converts vector data into raster. Attribute information is then assigned to each one of the cells or pixels in the grid, which forms the raster image. A uniform raster grid helps analyze the density of crime within irregular political boundaries. Using uniform grids of raster data, smaller localized crime hotspots within larger administrative and political boundaries may be identified by counting the number of occurrences within the area. The increased precision of smaller grids provides an advantage over the choropleth approach to crime mapping and an opportunity to focus resources on a particular rather than general problem area.

One example of this method is found on the CrimeMapper website of the Portland (OR) Police Department at http://www.portlandpolicebureau.com/. CrimeMapper is a web-based GIS program displaying crime density in the city of Portland. The interface for the software first asks for a street number and address, then it uses quarter-mile square grids as an overlay and counts the number of crimes by type occurring within the grid so the unit of analysis for the maps is crime per quarter mile. Next, CrimeMapper uses a choropleth display for the crime density data within the quarter-mile grids. The display is colorcoded and separated by the type of crime. The Portland Police Department provides one full year of data for the crimes of assault, arson, burglary, larceny, vehicle theft, robbery, sexual assault, and homicide. Additionally, the department updates the website on a monthly basis.

Density-Surface Mapping

A third method of analyzing and displaying crime density is to create a density-surface map showing variation over a geographic region.[3] For example, the density of a crime

such as personal robbery may be high in the center of a particular neighborhood and then drop off as one moves to its
edge. To analyze the concentration of crime, an analyst may
incorporate graduated colors as well as contour lines into a
density-map display.

Most GIS software packages allow the analyst to select
from a variety of data classification methods to display
graduated colors. Some of these methods include:

- Natural breaks, where the cell ranges are based on grouping data so that homogeneity within groups and heterogeneity between groups is maximized.
- Quantiles, where the same number of grid cells or other
  observations are in each data classification.
- Equal intervals that display the same difference between
  the high and low values of each classification.
- Standard deviation, which displays the classifications
  based on the standard deviation of the mean for all the
  data values. It is useful for highlighting extreme values.

Another method of displaying density information is to
use GIS software to create contour lines by connecting cells
with similar density values. The resulting contour lines look
very similar to lines on a topological map connecting areas
of similar elevation. In terms of data classification, the number of contour lines is determined by the contour interval
between the lines. If the contour interval is too small, then a
rapid change in a crime rate may be obscured. Likewise, if
the contour interval is too large, a small change in crime becomes imperceptible.

One of the shortcomings of many GIS software packages
is their limited statistical capability, especially in the area of
spatial statistics. Applying more sophisticated statistical
techniques to crime data requires additional software that
works in conjunction with the GIS. Certain spatial statistics
algorithms are more capable of detecting small variations in
crime than GIS techniques mentioned here. For crime
density-analysis, these techniques include one- and two-

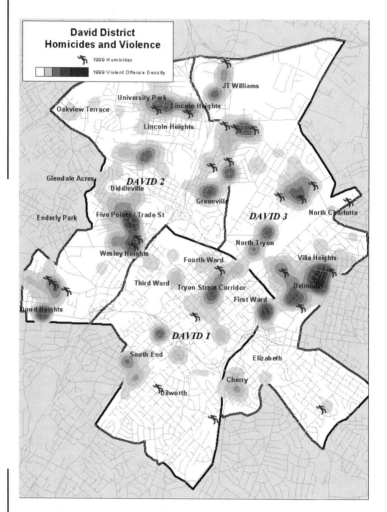

FIGURE 2.4 Hotspot Analysis of Homicides and Drug Arrests. *Matthew White, Charlotte-Mecklenburg Police Department; used with permission.*

kernel density interpolation. One-kernel density analysis is used to estimate the density of a single event across an entire region. For example, the estimated density of commercial burglary may be high in the center of a city and fall away rapidly outside the city. Two-kernel density analysis is used to examine incidents in relation to other variables such as population. Statistical methods such as these presently represent the "cutting edge" in using computerized crime mapping to understand crime density.

Creating Briefng Maps

One of the strengths of a GIS is its ability to communicate information visually. Since GIS has become more integrated into crime analysis, maps have begun moving from the wall of the police department into the hands of the front-line officers. Creating briefing maps for officers allows them to share the strategic view of crime analysts and police managers. Briefing maps are an important part of the crime-mapping process. Some 94 % of police departments using computerized crime mapping do so in order to keep detectives and officers informed about crime incidents. As a sergeant in the Charlotte-Mecklenburg, North Carolina Police Department noted:

> GIS maps give us information on what we think we know, but what it tells us a lot of times is what's going on when we're not working. The thing that officers have to remember is that for their eight hours a day, they may know what's going on in that response area or in that neighborhood. They're also not working 16 hours a day and two days off a week, and they may be on vacation. So to get a more global picture of what's going on in a neighborhood or geographic area, the maps . . . tell us, a lot of times, that our assumptions aren't necessarily what we thought they were.

One of the strengths of a GIS is that maps are dynamic and not static documents, updated instantly when the data changes. Geographic information systems provide a method to tailor maps for particular audiences. Within the police command structure, there may be different levels of detail required on a map depending on whether one is a patrol officer, investigator, or manager. Additionally, maps shared with the public through community meetings require tailoring for a special audience. Tailoring a briefing map does not, however, mean censoring the map.

Sharing Information

The COP and POP models advocate two-way information sharing between the public and police agencies. Briefing maps distributed to citizens and even Internet crime map sites are becoming important tools for sharing information. In a survey of police departments using computerized crime mapping, 82% of them also use the Internet. Harries (1999) identified three broad categories of maps used in community-oriented policing: crime and offender information, demographic information, and community and government resources. The full context of community-oriented policing and mapping will be discussed in a later chapter. Two of the broad categories useful as citizen briefing maps are maps of crime and offender information along with community and government resources.

One of the major questions about crime and offender information many citizens have is: "How much crime is in my neighborhood?" Likewise, citizens moving to a new city ask, "How much crime is in the neighborhood where I am interested in moving?" Crime and offender information is useful to inform residents about repeat crime activity as well as changes in their neighborhood. Disseminated either through the Internet or through other public channels, crime and offender information is useful for answering the question "Where is crime located?" The Tucson, Arizona, Police Department provides many of its routine maps on the Internet in order to more efficiently answer these types of questions.

Officers assigned to neighborhood watch and other crime prevention programs also use GIS crime maps to inform citizens of the actual locations of crime in their neighborhood. This type of briefing has two advantages: (1) it shows citizens where crime is actually located versus where they believe it's located and (2) it serves as an opportunity for a police department to demonstrate to the public its effectiveness in combating crime. After all, as many agencies have noted, if the police department does not provide crime information, some other source might do it and bias it with their interpretation.

Wartell and McEwen (2001) identify several more advantages departments gain from providing maps to the general public. Accurate data can encourage better community and police collaboration as citizens may become invested in cleaning up crime, especially if they see results of their anti-crime efforts on a map. Providing maps to the general public may increase their awareness of where crime is located. Increased awareness may bring increased funding or resources to a high crime area by mobilizing public opinion. There is a realization in law enforcement that "crime does not stop at the jurisdiction line." Briefing maps may help to facilitate data sharing with other local agencies such as public housing, colleges, or regional planning commissions. The desire to "stay ahead" may increase the numbers and types of maps provided under the category of operations and intelligence. Finally, briefing maps may increase police accountability by generating the need for officers to be just as informed about crime as the public at large.

Briefng Maps and Privacy Issues

There are many concerns related to privacy issues when placing crime maps on the Internet or providing them in a public forum. One concern for the law enforcement community is for the confidentiality of crime victims. By supplying data for a map, it may become easy to guess from the location of a crime the identity of a sexual assault victim, for instance. Accurately presenting data in briefing maps or on the Internet may be a function of finding a compromise between the citizen's right to know and the victim's right to privacy.

Another concern about providing police data in publicly available maps is that offenders might move to other areas in an elaborate game of cat and mouse. In fact, at a presentation to county sheriffs, one of the authors was presented with the following observation, "If we put crime maps on the Internet, then criminals will know our patrol tactics."

Commercialization of public data generates another potential issue with police briefing maps. Private security agencies may use the data as a marketing device to sell their products to home or business owners. Although marketing is a perfectly legal profession, the issue of using briefing maps arises from data interpretation. One of the hazards of using and interpreting choropleth maps is that a small section of an area may influence the information mapped for the entire boundary area. Thus a private security agency may use maps to do a mass mailing to everyone in a census tract highlighting a burglary problem that only exists in one particular section of the tract. Likewise, similar misinterpretation may lead to fears of an effect on property values by portraying a whole section of town as crime ridden when only one block has a crime problem.

Summary

Computerized crime mapping encompasses a hierarchy of basic operations, ranging from relatively simple to complex. It begins with pin mapping, an operation learned and applied quickly by novice users. Pin mapping is a gateway function to more complex crime-mapping functions. By creating pin maps, an agency develops basic mapping skills in preparation to explore more complex types of crime mapping.

Crime-density maps are a common transition from simple pin maps. These maps use graduated symbols as well as color intensity to indicate crime density. Choropleth maps use color intensity to indicate crime density in a boundary area. Because the data are aggregated, a choropleth map does not display the precise location of crime but assigns the density to the entire boundary area.

Hotspot analysis in crime mapping supports the transition of police operations from reactive to proactive strategies. One of the key functions of crime mapping is determining the hotspots of crime within a community. However, crime analysts as well as scholars all have slightly different definitions of what a hotspot is. Hotspot identification ranges from visually identifying the hotspots to using software with spatial statistics algorithms. In many respects it is more complicated than pin mapping or choropleth mapping. Determining the location of crime hotspots is the first step in understanding why certain crimes occur repeatedly in a particular area. The next step is to devise enforcement strategies and then monitor their progress.

Briefing maps are a crime-mapping product used by police departments to communicate internally as well as with the public. Briefing maps are used to communicate with citizens in community meetings to visually illustrate the status of crime and police efforts to combat it. Internally, police departments now use briefing maps to monitor crime, set management goals, and develop enforcement strategies.

Questions

1. What is pin mapping?
2. Why is pin mapping the "gateway" to more complicated crime mapping analysis?
3. Identify some of the criteria used to define a "hotspot."
4. Identify and describe the five techniques used for hotspot analysis.
5. What is choropleth mapping? Describe five methods of analyzing crime using density analysis.
6. Describe the benefits to a police department of using briefing maps in a community watch meeting.

CHAPTER 3

Managing Crime with Spatial Tools

Orthophotographic Mapping

Aerial photography is one method of gathering information by remote sensing.[1] The digital orthophotograph has broad applicability in computerized crime mapping. Orthophotography is the process of removing any distortions in an image caused by taking photographs from an airplane. The distortions in aerial photography are caused by the tilt of the airplane as well as the altitude differential of man-made and topological features. An aerial photograph is rectified into an orthophotograph by removing these distortions. After this process, the new image may be assigned the same spatial coordinates, attributes, or projections as a map.

300   0   300   600 Meters

FIGURE 3.1 Orthophotograph of downtown Raleigh, North Carolina. *Illustration created by author.*

Assigning spatial coordinates and projections allows the image to be used either as another theme in a map or a backdrop to visually enhance a GIS analysis. Most GIS software programs have utilities for projecting as well as adding coordinates to a raster image. Harries (2001) notes a broad range of information that may be added to an orthophotographic image. Possible data include census data, political boundaries, crime data, police districts and beats.

Most maps created from vector data are essentially abstractions of real life, lacking a certain level of depth and context. For example, a street centerline map does not show the type of buildings lining the street. Adding polygons can improve the map, allowing for representations of building footprints and other solid features. However, abstractions provide limited information for certain types of police operations such as special weapons and tactics (SWAT) or surveillance that may require a high level of detail about a particular area. Officers using Baltimore County

Police Department's mapping system listed digital orthophotographs as one of the top three choices for additional
map information.

Suppose a particular address is characterized by nuisance calls or repeated robberies where the offender easily
flees the police. Conventional crime mapping with a line
representation of the streets may not display escape avenues such as alleys or footpaths. By adding a digital orthophotograph as a backdrop to a conventional GIS map, officers responding to the call may see the other avenues
invisible in the conventional map. A recent study in Baltimore County (MD) demonstrated that maps and photographs used by themselves were not sufficient for understanding the context of a crime, but when used together
they created a synergistic effect of greater understanding
for the officers in the sample.[2] Crime analysts seeking to
understand a series of crimes will also have a more complete view of a problem area by using orthophotographs in
conjunction with GIS maps.

One example of using of digital orthophotography at the
tactical operating level was demonstrated by the Upland,
California, police department. The department's SWAT team
conducted a 4-hour practice drill at Upland High School centered on a hostage-taking scenario. Using digital orthophotography in conjunction with GIS, the SWAT team was able
to accurately visualize the school campus including the location of the hostages with portable laptop computers and GIS
software. The team was able to overlay different layers of information about the campus including detailed orthophotographs of the target building. These information sets and
the GIS program allowed the SWAT team to react much
faster to the hostage situation with less time spent on physical reconnaissance of the area.

Buffering and Proximity Analysis

Buffering and proximity analysis are two of the five general
functions of the spatial analysis component in GIS software.

Both are basic GIS functions widely used in crime mapping for elementary spatial analysis of crime. In GIS software, buffering actions draw concentric circles or polygons around a point of interest. For example, as part of a community policing initiative a police department might want to delineate a 1,000-foot drug-and weapons-free zone around a school. Within the zone a crime analyst might perform a proximity analysis by counting the numbers and types of crimes within the buffered distance. The relationship of crime and place is an important issue of study, as many types of crimes appear to have a distance aspect to them. As another example, the Bureau of Justice Statistics has noted that most violent crimes occur at or near the victim's home with half of these crimes occurring within a mile of the victim's home.[3] Garson and Biggs (1992) define the ability to relate map features to a dependent variable as spatial proximity analysis.

One well-known theory in criminal justice with "place" as a central feature is called routine activity theory. The central concept of routine activity theory is that the characteristics of certain places provide the opportunity for offenders to find either their victims or another opportunity to commit a crime. For example, pedophiles might find their victims at a school bus stop or even at the school itself simply because more victims are available in these particular locations. As a precaution, a crime analyst might buffer these sites and then monitor for the presence of any parolees or ex-offenders who begin living within the buffer zone. By using routine activity theory in conjunction with computerized crime mapping, repeat crimes within certain distances of a particular location might indicate the presence of a hotspot and the need for broader interventions.

Crime and Place

Since GIS has become a tool for analyzing crime, there have been correlational studies of different types of crimes and their proximity to various locations such as offender addresses, retail outlets, transit stations, and so on. Many of the cities that began using computerized crime mapping early have been studying the proximity relationship between crimes and geographic locations. Chief Statistician of the Baltimore County Police, Phil Canter, notes that:

> We look at the relationship between where an offense occurs and where the offender's last known place of residence was, and then we construct a function that describes how far they would travel to commit a crime. We use that as a guideline to extract out suspects. So we know, for instance, for firearm robberies, there's so many percent of all offenders that live within about six and a half miles of an offense location, so if you take a composite buffer that's six and a half miles from an offense location, there's a good chance that the offender lives within that area.

Buffering and proximity analysis serve as gateway functions for more sophisticated analyses of crime incidents. Before any intervention begins, one of the essential questions for crime analysts is determining whether the events within a buffered area are random or part of a hotspot.[4] To answer this question, analysts use a variety of spatial statistics techniques such as nearest-neighbor analysis, standard deviation ellipses, or distance decay. Although these techniques are not a complete list, they are a progression from simple counting and are logical building blocks for buffering and proximity analysis.

Nearest-neighbor analysis is used to identify groups of incidents that are closer in proximity to each other than expected by random chance. Nearest-neighbor analysis is an initial indicator that there is a relationship between a place and a particular set of events. The key issue of the analysis is locating the underlying place or cause generating the events. For example, a series of abandoned or stolen cars collected in an area may indicate the presence of a stolen-goods operation or a vehicle "chop shop." Similarly, repeated after-hours alcohol arrests in a neighborhood may indicate the presence of an illegal liquor establishment.

Another spatial method building on buffering and proximity analysis is the use of standard deviation ellipses. Standard deviation ellipses are computed by finding the geographic mean of a group of events and then computing a 68%, 95%, or even a 99% elliptically shaped probability area for finding similar events. Crime analysts use this as one method to forecast the probability areas for serial types of crimes. Harries (1999) notes the successful use of a standard deviation "box" calculated by the Los Angeles Police Department to forecast the probable operating area of the Los Angeles "Motorcycle Bandit." In the stolen-car example in the previous paragraph, the geographic locations of the abandoned cars may be used to generate a probability ellipse of locating the chop shop.

Distance decay refers to an inverse relationship such that as the distance from a point becomes greater, the number or type of incidents decrease. Block and Block (2000) compared actual and attempted robberies in the vicinity of public transportation transit stations in the Bronx (NY) and Chicago's northeast side. In each of the studies, Block and Block found a distance decay function beginning within a short distance of the transit station. The zones of highest attempts and actual robberies were found to vary between 700 and 1,000 feet from the transit stations. Using knowledge of crime and distance decay can help analysts to focus intervention on the actual nexus of a problem.

As computerized crime analysis has evolved beyond simple pin mapping, software packages have been written to perform various spatial analyses of crime. Software analysis packages vary in availability from sophisticated software from commercial vendors to freeware developed under Department of Justice contracts. Many of these packages work in conjunction with leading GIS software such as ArcView or MapInfo.[5] In pursuing the connection between crime and place, researchers are exploring more spatial statistics techniques to isolate and identify nonrandom clusters of crime. Although the relationship between crime and place appears to be important, Anselin et al. (2000) note the actual connection between the two is not known. The authors also note that despite being a very promising tool, location should not be relied on exclusively for crime control.

Resource Allocation with Crime Mapping

One of the common administrative procedures within police departments is to divide the jurisdiction into manageable chunks called districts or precincts, which are then subdivided into smaller areas designated as patrols or beats. At the operations level, districting makes allocation of police resources more manageable, and it dovetails with the command structure of the police force. For example, a police captain who is ultimately responsible for activity in the area usually commands a district and the resources assigned to it. In the days before GIS these districts were often established arbitrarily by drawing imaginary lines using easy-to-identify landmarks to delineate the boundaries. It is possible that police districts may have even been established early in a city's life and have the weight of custom behind them rather than being based on any data about the distribution of crime.

A major issue in police work is that over time criminal activity shifts in response to enforcement, economic, demographic, or other factors. Depending on the jurisdiction, these shifts might occur annually or over a period of some years. Developing a redistricting plan for a police department is not as simple as erasing and redrawing the lines. Usually redrawing police districts is an issue of morale among the officers as well as the politics of command. Although there is no formal study regarding traditional redistricting, anecdotal evidence suggests it has been a time and labor-intensive process for the participants. Geographic information systems technology gives a police department the ability to realign the old or even establish new police districts far more easily and quickly, based on arrest and activity data or calls for service. In previous research by the au-

thors, we noted that Charlotte-Mecklenburg, North Carolina, police department credits GIS technology with com-
pleting the redistricting process faster:

> Through the redistricting effort that we did, GIS enabled us to
> use a number of different data sources that we hadn't used in
> the past and did it in a more effective manner, and we were
> also more efficient because we cut down on the number of
> hours that it actually took . . . we basically sat in a room with all
> the district captains and in one day, accomplished what took
> two people six to nine months to accomplish in the past.

Creating Administrative Boundaries

One of the first steps in allocating resources is to establish
some type of administrative framework. Most police departments divide a city into districts or precincts. However
these are arbitrary administrative boundaries and may be
changed in response to a department's needs. Geographic
information system technology allows a user to create, edit,
and display boundaries on a base map. Three options available for creating administrative boundaries are to conform
the districts to existing neighborhood boundaries, use zip
codes and census tracts, or create new districts based on
crime incident or arrest data.

• Neighborhood Boundaries
Base maps of neighborhood boundaries can be created using
vector data in a GIS. One method is to create boundaries using
an existing city map as a backdrop and then create the boundaries as a new file using the on-screen digitizing capability
available in most GIS software packages. The San Diego Police
Department is an example of a department allocating resources and officers based on established neighborhood areas
as part of their community-oriented policing philosophy.

• Census Tracts and Zip Codes
To effectively allocate resources it may be helpful to have access to a variety of social and demographic data to supple-

ment other data. Two types of boundaries with demographic data that are readily available from commercial software sources are census tracts and zip codes. A major source for this information is the U.S. Census Bureau, which collects socio-demographic information by census tracts and provides several characteristics useful for resource allocation. Census tracts are designed to be stable over time, as homogeneous in population as possible, and contained within existing political boundaries.[6]

• Past Arrest Data and Calls for Service

After establishing police boundaries, one method for deciding where to allocate resources is to map criminal activity with a choropleth map. Two types of data are readily available for mapping crime history and call-for-service data. A choropleth map is useful for displaying density within boundaries, and it assigns a single value to the entire boundary area. As an option, police managers might use the mapped data to shift the major allocation of assets to the highest crime or calls for service areas. However, an issue with allocating services in this manner is one of proper balance or perspective. Although some areas may have more crimes or calls for service, they might be less severe, requiring fewer resources to resolve them. One resolution to this issue is to systematically assign weights to various crimes before mapping and making decisions about moving resources.

Software Solutions

Geographic information systems technology can speed up and simplify the process of realigning or creating police districts. The two major software packages used in crime analysis, ArcView by ESRI[7] and MapInfo,[8] both have redistricting extensions as part of their GIS software. Although the extensions were primarily designed for voting redistricting, they are easily adapted for crime mapping. Both packages allow the use of geographic boundaries such as census tracts, zip codes, and so on as the background information for creating new districts.

In order to use the redistricting extensions, the user needs a geographic as well as an information file. The geographic file contains the boundary information, and the information file contains the calls for service or other workload data. The information file must have a common field with the geographic file in order to join the two. For example, if an analyst is using census tracts as the geographic boundary in order to link workload data to geographic data, both files must have a common field like the census tract number. Both software packages allow the user to specify an optimal number of districts in a process known as workload balancing. Additionally, the user can manually adjust the affiliation of any districts during the workload-balancing process. Baltimore County's Police Department[9] used MapInfo's Redistricting extension and credited it with a 92% savings in time by compressing the reallocation process from 100 weeks to 8 weeks.

Mapping and Community-Oriented Policing

Community-oriented policing and problem-oriented policing are shifts from previous approaches to policing that were prevalent from the 1960s to the 1980s. Police methods in those years were more reactive to crime as they focused on response times to calls for service, enforcing laws, and random patrolling in police cruisers. By the 1970s there was widespread professional dissatisfaction with these methods. Community-oriented policing as a major shift in police operations evolved from efforts to bring the police and community closer together. Often the terms COP and POP are used interchangeably, but criminologists and police scholars make a definite distinction between the two based on their fundamental philosophy.

Community-oriented policing is best characterized as collaboration between the public and police to reduce crime at the neighborhood level. Police departments practicing

COP reach out to include the community as part of their overall strategy in combating crime. There is no precise definition of COP; however, it is usually considered an overall philosophy to guide police departments rather than as a special section within it. The major shift in community-oriented policing involves a broader definition of police work, which involves activities such as:

- Identifying the full range of problems experienced by community residents.
- Working with community residents to develop strategies for addressing those problems.
- Bringing in the appropriate public and nonprofit agencies to implement those strategies.

The lack of precise definition allows the implementation of COP to take on different forms. One of the major interpretations is a return to more personal contact between the community and police. For example, many departments interpret COP as a return to the neighborhood police officer whom everyone knows and who is completely familiar with the neighborhood. Personal contact can take other forms also: foot patrols, neighborhood watch groups, bicycle patrols, and so on. Most of these methods put officers in closer contact with the community by removing them from the isolation of a patrol car. A more familiar relationship between the police and the community is considered essential for collaboration on other problems. Geographic information systems play a role in COP by providing beat maps of neighborhoods and also displaying neighborhood crime trends for community outreach meetings.

Problem-Oriented Policing

Herman Goldstein, in the 1970s, was the first to propose a new method he called problem-oriented policing. Problem-oriented policing has three goals: to identify crimes specifically rather than in broad legal terms, to collect information about problems from a variety of sources, including outside the police department, and to seek broad solutions to the problem including alternatives to the criminal justice system. Geographic information systems play a role in POP by providing maps of specific crime distributions and trends, and map overlays and spatial statistics that relate risk factors to rate of crime occurrence.

As both concepts have developed, POP is discriminated from COP by an emphasis on analytical, police-centered decision-making. Community-oriented policing and POP may use some of the same techniques, but in the POP model, collaboration with the community is not necessarily the first option to solving a problem but exists within a range of possible responses. Problem-oriented policing does not seek responsibility for broader, sociological solutions to crime that COP strives for, rather, it remains centered on how police departments can specifically respond to crime problems within their mandate.

How Does Crime Mapping Aid Community-Oriented Policing?

Rohe (2001) identifies three levels of community-oriented policing: the philosophical, the program, and the activity level. Crime mapping is a critical tool linking all three levels. The philosophical level involves how the entire department adopts the principles of community-oriented policing. In other words, will COP be treated as a significant shift in doing police business, or will it be treated as an annoying mandate or a fad? The program level is where police departments make certain choices in implementing COP, such as where and how to apply it. There are no "formula" applications in COP, only a common focus on proactive rather than reactive policing; therefore implementation of COP varies across the country. At this level, based on the guiding principles of COP, community officers are free to determine the most effective method of getting to know their community at the front line in direct contact with citizens.

At the program level, police departments want to determine where to apply COP. Crime mapping as an analytical tool aids departments at the program and activity level to identify communities that may benefit from the COP approach. At the activity level, crime mapping helps patrol officers view the community in relation to its surrounding environment. Harries (1999) proposes three general categories of useful information to map for COP: crime and offender information, community and government resources, and demographics. At the program level, all three categories are useful in determining where to apply COP. Both demographic and crime and offender information are variables departments will use in determining where to focus a COP initiative. Because one of the principles of COP is to collaborate in finding community solutions to problems, mapping available resources is also useful at the program level as a lack of certain resources may indicate a greater need for a COP initiative.

Patrol officers working at the activity level benefit from having crime maps to share with community or neighborhood watch groups. One of the most instructive briefings officers can give a community is to show where crime is actually located versus where citizens think it is located. Reducing fear is one the basic reasons for bringing police and the community together. Demographic information in maps is also useful to officers assigned to community areas, giving them an opportunity to understand the various populations they will be serving. Finally, offender and parolee information in maps is useful to patrol officers in pursuing crime leads.

A good example of integrating GIS into the COP model is the city of San Diego. In 1994 San Diego reorganized its police department by aligning police beats with neighborhoods. In addition to this realignment, front-line patrol officers were brought into more contact with crime analysts. The increased contact allowed patrol officers to get the "bigger picture" of crime in their neighborhoods. In addition to bringing the strategic level and front line together, the San Diego Police Department also brought business owners and residents together as part of the problem-solving process. San Diego has experienced a significant drop in violent crimes as well as burglaries, assaults, and auto thefts. San Diego's crime statistics from 1950 to 2000 are available on-line at http://www.sannet.gov/police/pdf/sdhcr00.pdf.

In this section we explored the application of computerized crime mapping to two of the prevailing theories in police operations, COP as well as POP. Both approaches have a common focus on proactive rather than reactive police work using crime mapping as an analytical tool to design responses to crime. In the case of COP, the response involves bringing the community into the process of seeking solutions for crime problems. On the other hand, POP seeks community input only if it is necessary to solving a crime problem. Both COP and POP use crime mapping as an analytic tool for strategic decision-making about resource allocation and for tactical support of police operations in the field.

Summary

Computerized crime mapping supports community policing efforts by helping crime analysts identify crime hotspots within their communities. Managing crime with GIS requires using certain spatial tools that include but are not limited to:

• Orthophotography
• Real-time response mapping
• Buffering and proximity mapping
• Resource allocation

Orthophotography is the process of removing distortions from aerial photography. Aerial photographs are useful for identifying surface change anomalies that may indicate a crime scene. Digital orthophotographs used in a GIS enhance the legibility of crime maps by providing recognizable reference points for analysts as well as officers.

Real-time response mapping is at the cutting edge of computerized crime mapping. To map in real time, a data link must exist between the crime-mapping and records-management systems. Presently, agencies using this method typically have a delay between receiving the reports and transmitting them to crime analysts and officers, but in the future crime reports entered at the scene may be available to update maps instantly.

Buffering and proximity mapping are two GIS functions widely used in crime mapping. The buffering function allows an analyst to query within a known distance of a geographic point. For example, establishing concentric rings around a school, a sports arena, and so on are all examples of buffering. Proximity mapping includes identifying the number and type of events within a certain distance from the point of interest.

Police departments have begun using computerized crime mapping to allocate patrol resources as well as to create new districts. The major GIS software manufacturers have adapted programs for determining voting districts that help allocate police resources. Geographic information system technology replaces pen, paper, and persuasion with a more rational and data-driven process of resource allocation, resulting in dramatic time savings and efficiencies.

Questions

1. What is orthophotography and why is it useful in crime mapping?
2. When might buffering be used in crime mapping?
3. Explain "routine activity theory" and its relation to proximity analysis.
4. What are standard deviation ellipses used for in crime mapping?
5. Explain the three possible bases of law enforcement jurisdiction redistricting using GIS tools.
6. Explain how GIS may provide important support for the community-oriented policing model.

CHAPTER 4

Modeling Crime with Spatial Tools

Spatial Situational and Historical Analysis

Spatial situational analysis is the analysis of types of crime by types of setting. For example, crime mapping may focus on analysis of crime in abandoned buildings, in establishments serving liquor, in high schools, and overlaying setting maps to understand possible interaction of settings. Spatial situational analysis includes target profiling as in comparing convenience store locations with actual convenience store robberies. Thus the Lenexa, Kansas, Police Department applied spatial situational analysis to construction sites:

We had a big problem with construction site theft, and so we plotted the locations of the sites that had already been hit, then went into our building permit files, in the Planning Department, and overlaid all the permits that had been issued. We did some surveillance on the sites that hadn't been hit yet, and were able to capture the folks as a result of that. (Garson and Vann 2001: 42)

Similarly, the city of Wilson, North Carolina, used situational analysis successfully to stake out targets and apprehend criminals when it had a problem with crime in abandoned buildings, and again when it had a problem with crime in churches.

School-related crime is a common focus for situational analysis in crime mapping (Feliciano 2001). The National Institute of Justice has developed and distributes software called School Crime Operations Package as a resource for improving school collection of crime incident data (Rich 2001). Collecting incident data allows schools to map the occurrence of crime at or adjacent to schools, prioritize safety problems, select among the many response strategies (e.g., video cameras, metal detectors, conflict-resolution classes), and evaluate if these strategies actually reduced school-related crime.

Other jurisdictions, like Upland, California, have taken a proactive stance regarding school-related crime, using GIS technology. A major problem reflected in the Columbine High School tragedy, in which two teens murdered class members in a carefully orchestrated attack, was that due to absence of floor plans for the school, response was delayed by 46 minutes. Upland reacted by creating a GIS-based updatable CD-ROM that provides police and other authorities with complete interactive information not only about the floor plans (drawn directly from computer-assisted design building plans) but also data on attributes of each room, location of fire alarm controls (deafening noise had hampered response at Columbine), controls for sprinkler systems, lighting switches, aerial photographs of the school and surroundings, personnel information, and much more, all instantly retrievable. Moreover, this geodatabase was combined with contingency planning for establishment of possible police command posts within the school, planned exit routes for escaping students, and other tactical information. The former system's reliance on outdated three-ring planning binders with partial information stored in a police department file cabinet was replaced by a modern GIS in which crime-mapping information was closely integrated with tactical plans, issued in a CD-ROM format that was both much more comprehensive in terms of data, much more useful in terms of access, and much more timely because it could easily be widely copied and distributed to all essential personnel. A similar system has been implemented by the Critical Incident Management Unit of the San Diego Police Department, using a geodatabase that can be delivered via the World Wide Web or, delivered to mobile computing units using ESRI ArcExplorer map viewer (Bowman-Jamieson and Smith 2001).

A different type of situational analysis looks at schools in relation to drug arrests. The San Diego Police Department tracks drug information (drug-related citizen complaints and calls for service, narcotics arrests) and displays it for analysis on a map that shows 1,000-foot buffers around schools, highlighting drug activity in school zones (Smith 2001). Mapping allows clusters of drug points to be identified quickly and easily as a prelude to developing countermeasures. Maps also provide useful up-to-the minute information for police offers walking patrol beats. Map overlays of drug points also can be compared to overlays for other types of crime to identify criminal modes of operation. Likewise, map drug-point overlays for a given week may be compared to those for data for past weeks, adding a dynamic element to analysis of emerging patterns.

There are numerous other examples of situational spatial analysis with regard to school-related crime. School-related crime is associated with "unowned" spatial areas not ordinarily supervised by adults, and these can be mapped for patrol and response purposes (Astor, Meyer, and Behre 1999). Some schools are more prone to repeat vandalism than others, and GIS databases can easily identify and map repeats for purposes of revising patrol assignments (Burquest, Farrell, and Pease 1992). In general, crime mapping can easily spotlight the distribution of the risk factors for school crime, whether the spatial distribution of poverty in a community, the distribution of youth gangs' "turf," the distribution of handgun ownership, the location of street lighting, and so on, and the overlay of risk factors on school maps helps communities and decision-makers develop efficient and effective response strategies.

Spatial Historical Analysis

Spatial historical analysis is the relationship of recurring non-crime events such as sporting events, political rallies, festivals, and so on to crime. Take, for example, a major event in a city such as a football game or a rock concert. Depending on the circumstances, such an event may generate increased arrests for alcohol or property-damage incidents surrounding the stadium. An example of this relationship is usually seen whenever international soccer teams enter the World Cup phase of competition. Based on prior experience with exuberant soccer fans, the countries hosting the event tend to reinforce the capabilities of their police, anticipating increased rowdy behavior or hooliganism.

A survey by the authors found very few police departments extensively using this method of analysis. However, one department that reported successfully using this method was the Chicago Police Department in conjunction with the NBA championship games played by the Chicago Bulls in the mid-1990s. Since the team won the championship several years in a row, the police department was able to use historical crime data based on past experience with the event to effectively allocate police resources. In the authors' interviews, other departments where large stadiums or entertainment complexes are located were beginning to explore using spatial historical analysis as part of their contingency planning for major events.

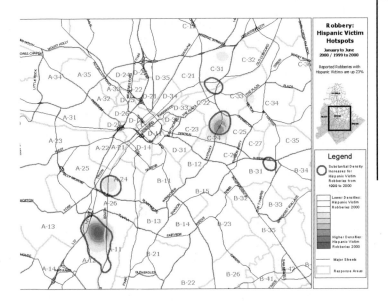

FIGURE 4.1 Spatial Historical Analysis of Robbery Victim Hotspots. *Matthew White, Charlotte-Mecklenburg Police Department; used with permission.*

Multivariate Pattern Analysis

A major use of crime-mapping tools is to relate the pattern of a type of offense to the complex web of social, environmental, and institutional factors that affect crime, in order to understand crime as a process for purposes of strategic law enforcement planning. Spatial analysis has been used over the last few decades to study many dimensions of crime, including drug trafficking (Eck 1995), gambling (Hakim and Buck 1989), serial rape (Lebeau 1992), auto theft (Ley and Cybriwsky 1974), homicide (Alexander and Xiang 1994), even campus crime (O'Kane, Fisher, and Green 1994), to name a few. Crime pattern analysis is now routinely covered in manuals for police support units (e.g., Openshaw, Waugh, Cross, Brunsdon, and Lillie 1991).

Multivariate pattern analysis takes not only crime into account but also social, cultural, economic, and even physical variables related to the community. Law enforcement planners can use multivariate information not just to respond to crime tactically but also to understand some of the root causes of particular types of crimes. Understanding root causes, in turn, makes community policing a more meaningful strategy and enables closer cooperation with neighborhoods seeking to attack drug markets, reduce convenience store crime, or engage in other law enforcement operations.

To illustrate pattern analysis, a crime-mapping project on homicides in the District of Columbia, New Orleans, and Richmond examined the presence of historical hotspots and/or the changes in hotspot locations at the block-group level, relating homicides to social and economic variables including poverty, percentage of young males age 16 to 24, type of housing, population density, employment rates, employment opportunities, and educational levels of population by race. Spatial aspects of homicide were studied, including churches, police units, community programs, bars, liquor stores, and known drug and gang territories.[1]

As a second example of multivariate pattern analysis, the Illinois State Policy analyzed risk factors of methamphetamine use. Indicators of methamphetamine use included data on stationary, mobile, abandoned, and box labs; seizures, purchases, dealers, and anhydrous ammonia thefts; and methamphetamine addict information from the Great River Recovery Resources and the Western States Intelligence Network. Using these indicators, researchers exploring GIS were able to show the spatial correlation of methamphetamine use with the following risk factors: percent of individuals 25 years old or more, having less than a high school diploma by census tract; percent of unmarried individuals over 25 years of age by census tract; increase or decrease in the crime rate by county; percent change in drug arrest rate by county; poverty rate by census tract; and residence in a rural county. To obtain the risk factors map, the state of Illinois was partitioned into a gridwork by Spatial Analyst, an extension to ArcView (a leading GIS package), and risk factors were summed for each grid cell, then displayed as a color ramp in which darker reds signified areas of higher risk. Risk mapping enabled more effective assignment of investigatory and enforcement personal in anti-methamphetamine law enforcement operations.

Crime analysis involves discerning patterns formed by multiple variables. Courses in criminal intelligence analysis cover how to establish links between people, organizations, and events; how to chart events, commodity flow, and activities within the criminal organization; and how money is laundered and stolen goods are "fenced." All of this involves understanding how to turn data into information, how to use the computer to assist the intelligence function, and how to distinguish among tactical, strategic, and operational intelligence. After intelligence is examined, analysts must also learn how to present it effectively in oral and written reports, how to construct and interpret scatter diagrams, frequency charts, time series analysis, data correlation charts, and other forms of data visualization. Crime mapping, because of its ability to include spatial as well as conventional crime variables, its ability to treat variables in separate layers, and its intuitive visual nature is a critical tool allowing the analyst to see patterns and then effectively communicate these patterns to decision makers.

Organizing Multivariate Crime Data

It is natural to organize crime data by reporting districts. However, precinct-size districts may cover multiple neighborhoods and when data are aggregated at the precinct level, patterns can become obscured. It is best if reporting districts (sometimes called grids or atoms) are small and do not change when precinct lines change. Census block groups make excellent reporting districts, typically covering about 1,000 residents or about 400 homes. Census blocks usually do not cut across physical or political boundaries and, from a mapping viewpoint, the data and boundary files are free from the U.S. Bureau of the census, which updates them regularly. Crime data using census blocks as reporting units can be merged easily with census demographic information, including variables on population, education, housing, employment, and other socioeconomic attributes of the block. Moreover, using census standard industry codes, one can add map themes related to the location of bars, liquor stores, and nightclubs/restaurants to be able to analyze problem establishments.[2]

Unfortunately, in the real world the geocoding (matching addresses of crime incidents to x, y coordinates on a map) of crimes location is not precise (*Crime Mapping News* 1999a). For this reason, multivariate pattern analysis may well use a *vicinity approach* to spatial data. In this approach, a circular buffer is drawn around apparent crime locations and then, instead of using just demographic or other variable information for the polygon (e.g., the census block) in which the crime is apparently located, the analyst uses the mean value of all polygons within the buffer. The use of such areally weighted averages of data in the immediate vicinity of the apparent location of the crime serves as a smoothing factor, improving the overall power and predictability of the statistical analysis of crime (Ratcliffe and McCullagh 1999).

Among the varied statistical techniques for multivariate analysis of crime are point-pattern analysis[3] (Boots and Getis 1988, Canter 1995), nearest neighborhood analysis (Block, Dabdoub, and Fregly 1995), and cluster analysis (Thill and Yang 1999). Rogerson and Sun (2001) describe a new procedure that utilizes the nearest-neighbor statistic and cumulative-sum methods to detect changes over time in the spatial pattern of point events, namely, 1996 arson data from the Buffalo Police Department.

Displaying Multivariate Crime Data

The capacity of crime maps to handle even more variables can be enhanced by using animation to represent an additional dimension such as change over time. Virtual Reality

Modeling Language (VRML) animations are one way to implement animated data visualization (Lodha and Verma 1999). Not only can a map be animated, but the analyst, decision-maker, or citizen user can examine a map by "flying" around or through it in a three-dimensional manner. Virtual reality modeling language maps can be rotated, tilted, and zoomed-in on to discern data patterns.[4] This converts the interpretation of map data from a passive to an active mode, with the viewer playing a creative role in data exploration. Police in Vancouver, British Columbia, have used VRML to depict various types of crimes.

Conditioned choropleth maps are a simpler way of representing multivariate data (Carr and Carr 2000). A choropleth map is an ordinary shaded map, such as a map of census districts shaded or colored according to the amount of some variable such as number of crimes of a given type. Normally choropleth maps represent just two dimensions: the spatial dimension and the dimension represented by one variable, such as number of property crimes. However, it is possible to create a matrix of a number of choropleth maps, where the row the map is in represents a second variable (in addition to the original choropleth variable such as the number of property crimes) and the column the map is in represents a third variable. For instance, the rows could represent blocks or other reporting areas with < $10,000 median income, $10,000–$25,000 median income, and > $25,000. Likewise, the columns could represent three levels of unemployment. Thus the map in the lower left cell of the matrix would depict number of property crimes for lowest-income, worst-unemployment areas The array as a whole is called a conditioned choropleth map, and viewing the set of maps it contains allows one to view not only number of crimes but also related forces such as neighborhood income level and unemployment in this example.[5] In a dynamic version of conditioned choropleth mapping, the user can select the row and column variables and explore relationships to property crime involving dozens of combinations of variables.

Spatial Modeling

Spatial modeling refers to a set of statistical techniques that operationalize theories of crime to make predictions. Some modeling techniques are computerized and go beyond depicting crime data on a static map but instead incorporate a time variable to implement a dynamic map, which, in computer simulation mode, can be "played" forward in time to forecast future patterns. Examples of spatial modeling techniques include systems theory modeling with Dynamo and other simulation languages (Kern 1989; Stull 1994), structural equation modeling, and neural network analysis (Caulkins, Cohen, and Wei 1996) as well as simpler modes such as criminal geographic targeting models described later.

Criminological models, also called *CGT models,* help police track serial offenders. Criminological modeling is a form of geographic profiling that rests on the assumption that there is a geographic relationship between where serial criminals have committed their crimes and where they live. Criminological models often start with identifying the location or probable location of a suspect's home. Geographic information systems staff can map these home addresses on one layer of a map, then overlay additional layers for suspect work addresses, establishments frequented by suspects, locations of past serial offense crimes, home addresses of victims of suspected serial criminals, work addresses of victims, and establishments frequented by victims. Examining the spatial intersections of suspect and victim locations of interest can reveal patterns that suggest how victims were selected and where future crimes may occur and can help police prioritize suspects.

Among the patterns criminological models look for are ones suggested by "routine activities theory": the expectation that crime occurs near places where criminals live, work, and shop and routes to and from these places (see Felson 1987). Routine activities theory suggests that serial offenders, like most of us, have routines involving shopping, traveling to work, visiting friends, and so on, and they become familiar with targets of opportunity that they notice in the course of these routine activities.

Alternatively, criminological models may test "environmental theory" (the expectation that crime occurs along well-identified paths, edges, nodes, and landmarks such as major grid-pattern streets, fringes such as riverfronts, nodes such as shopping centers, and landmarks such as railway stations. Developed by Simon Fraser University's School of Criminology and pioneered by Brantingham and Brantingham (1981, 1993), this version of criminologic modeling assumes (1) that serial criminals commit crimes within their routine activity areas but (2) do not commit crimes in the immediate area of their actual residences. Based on these two assumptions, CGT modeling software uses a distance-decay function to assign a residential probability to various areas on a map, giving police a priority list of potential locations where the criminal's residence may be found. A CGT map may be a "fishnet" surface map of an inner city, for instance, with the peaks on this surface representing the most likely locations of the criminal's residence. Alternatively, a two-dimensional map may be produced, with most likely residential locations shown in red (high probability) and yellow (secondary probability) (Rossmo 1995). Criminal geographic targeting methodology has been integrated in Rigel workstations, which integrate GIS with geographic profiling methodology. Based on geoprofiling, patrol officer maps are produced and distributed to show only the locations of the most likely residents of a suspect. Geoprofile maps may also be distributed through community policing or in the media to heighten public awareness and generate tips.

As a third alternative, criminological models may test "social disorganization theory" (the expectation that crime occurs in areas of high poverty, high unemployment, high mobility, high school dropout rates, and the like; see Shaw and McKay 1942; Bursik 1988). These patterns were tested using GIS, for instance, in analysis for Dover Township, New Jersey (Johnson 2000).

In a different sort of criminological model, the Los Angeles Police Department used simple means and standard deviation statistics to produce a map showing the 68% probability and 95% probability geographic boundaries within which the Los Angeles Motorcycle Bandit could be predicted to strike next. This simple model proved so useful that it was automated and distributed even outside the Los Angeles Police Department (Geggie 1998).

Spatiotemporal Clustering Models

Sometimes crime is unreported or may even be unapparent. For instance, the New York State Bureau of Arson used MapInfo GIS software to analyze a pattern of almost-daily crimes occurring in Utica, New York, in 1997. "Some city officials were not willing to admit that an arson problem existed until we showed them one year's [map] layer over previous years," Arson Bureau Deputy Chief Jim Brezzell noted. "Once the incendiary fires were shown on maps with red flame icons, it was hard to deny a problem" (Kelly 1999:6).

A dramatic case where crime was not apparent came to light in the instance of an English doctor who made a practice of murdering elderly female patients and may have been responsible for as many as 200 deaths, making him England's most prolific serial killer. Yet, because of the "natural" appearence of the deaths, it was not apparent for years that there was a crime problem at all. To deal with this sort of situation, crime analysts at the New Scotland Yard developed a "stealth predator model" that used GIS to track and map clusters of missing cases reports in order to identify nonrandom patterns warranting police investigation. Spatiotemporal clustering models are not limited to missing persons. At a more general level, such models use spatial-statistical tests to call attention to situations where "too many crimes are happening, in too short a time period, in too small an area" compared to historical benchmarks (Rossmo and Davies 2001: 7).

Spatiotemporal modeling is also useful for the analysis of crime series. A criminal may commit the same type of crime at the same time of day, over a period of weeks or months. A GIS can isolate crime incidents by these factors (type, time) and display them on a map with symbols indicating chronological sequence. This enables analysts to determine the "hunting ground" (the area in which the crimes are taking place), the distribution (dispersion of crimes within the hunting ground area), distance (the sequential distance of space from one case to the next), crawl (the movement of the area within the time span), dispersal (relationship of the spatial distribution to the time span), and spacing (the ratio of distance to interval between crimes in the series). The spatial mathematics of computing "hunting ground," "distance," "crawl," and other concepts is discussed in Helms (2000), who also provides illustrative maps. Spatiotemporal analysis allows crime mappers to make educated guesses about where, when, and how often crime incidents will occur in a given crime series.

Quasi-experimental Models

Although true experimentation is rarely, if ever, possible or ethical in social settings, it is possible to conduct quasi-experiments. In this method, one spatial area of interest is compared on one or more variables with control areas. An example is provided by Paul (2001). This study examined the hypothesis that exotic dance nightclubs in Fort Wayne, Indiana, attracted crime. Paul used GIS to establish a 1,000-foot buffer around each of eight exotic dance nightclubs in Fort Wayne and around eight comparison areas matched to the club areas on the basis of demographic features and commercial property composition. By comparing the number of calls for service (CFS rate) to the police from 1997 to 2000 in target nightclub areas and in the control areas, Paul was able to demonstrate that for these data there was no appreciable difference—that is, there was no significant negative secondary effect of adult businesses on crime and, therefore, no reason to allocate police resources disproportionately to these areas.

Ordinary Least-Squares Regression Modeling

Ordinary least-squares regression has long been used to analyze crime variables on a spatial basis. Multiple regression is used to account for (predict) the variance in an interval dependent variable such as amount of a certain kind of crime in a given patrol jurisdiction, based on linear combinations of causal variables. Multiple regression equations are prediction equations such that one may plug in "what-if" values for key causal variables, such as number of patrol officers, to predict what the effect might be on a key dependent variable, such as number of drug-related arrests (Geake 1993).

Spatial Regression and Spatial Econometric Modeling

Spatial regression analysis and related methods of spatial econometrics deal with issues of spatial dependence (variables related to crime are also related to location) and of spatial heterogeneity (variables related to crime vary in their dispersion across space). To take a hypothetical example, whereas ordinary regression might not show much relation between poverty of neighborhood and auto theft, spatial regression might show, for instance, that due to relative deprivation, poor neighborhoods near wealthy ones (but not poor neighborhoods in general) do exhibit a relation of poverty to auto theft. Economic models of crime are not new and, in fact, there is an entire academic field called "economic geography" (Brown 1982). Now spatial regression and spatial econometric techniques are increasingly common in social science in general, and criminology in particular.

Spatial autocorrelation has been the focus of a series of studies by French criminologist Daniel Elie (Elie and Legendre 1992; Elie 1994). Morenoff, Sampson, and Raudenbush (2001) used spatial regression to study violent behavior in urban neighborhoods. The authors found that concentrated social and economic disadvantage, along with low levels of social control and cohesion, predicted higher rates of homicide. They also found that the density of local organizations and voluntary associations mattered surprisingly little, while friend and kinship networks affected how well residents are able to generate social control and cohesion.

Multilevel Modeling

Multilevel modeling is a form of hierarchical regression analysis developed since the 1980s, designed to handle hierarchical and clustered data. Crime data involve neighborhood and other group effects on individuals that may be assessed invalidly by traditional regression techniques. That is, when grouping is present (e.g., crimes in precincts), observations within a group (a precinct, for instance) are often more similar than would be predicted on a pooled-data basis, and hence the statistical assumption of independence of observations is violated.

The traditional approach to multilevel problems was to aggregate data to a superlevel (e.g., crime data are averaged to the precinct level and precincts are used at the unit of analysis) or to disaggregate data to the base level (e.g., each crime is assigned various precinct-level variables such as prevailing force level, and all crimes in a given precinct have the same value on these contextual variables, and crimes are used as the unit of analysis). Ordinary least-squares regression or another traditional technique is then performed on the unit of analysis chosen. There were three problems with this traditional approach: (1) under aggregation, fewer units of analysis at the superlevel replace many units at the base level, resulting in loss of statistical power; (2) under disaggregation, information from fewer units at the superlevel is wrongly treated as if it were independent data for the many units at the base level, and this error in treating sample size leads to overoptimistic estimates of significance; and (3) under either aggregation or disaggregation, there is the danger of the ecological fallacy: there is no necessary correspondence between individual-level and group-level variable relationships.

Multilevel modeling uses variables at superlevels (e.g., force levels in precincts) to adjust the regression of base level (e.g., crime level) dependent variables on base-level independent variables (e.g., predicting type of crime type

from location of crime). Because hierarchical data are ex-
tremely common in law enforcement settings, multilevel
modeling is highly salient. Gottfredson (1991) is among
those who have used multilevel analysis to study social
area influences on juvenile delinquency, for instance.

Neural Network Modeling

Olligschlaeger (1997) utilized neural network analysis (a
form of statistical "artificial intelligence" used in forecasting; see Garson, 1998) in work with the Pittsburgh Police
Department to predict spatial patterns in drug transactions.
Drug markets were seen as an early warning indicator of
crime, since drug addiction is a crime generator for offenses
such as robberies and burglaries. Using weapon-related,
robbery, and assault calls-for-service data, along with variables on commercial land use and seasonality, Pittsburgh
was mapped onto a grid of cells (each a little over 2,000
square feet) Olligschlaeger demonstrated that the neural
model forecast the spatial distribution of crime more effectively than alternative statistical models.

In another application of neural network analysis, Corcoran and Ware (2001) have shown how this technique can be
used to cluster crime data in a way that brings to light
hitherto hidden information embedded in large spatial databases. Using a variant of neural network analysis, namely
Kohonen Self-Organizing Maps, the authors demonstrated
how a spatial probability matrix may be constructed to forecast that when certain ambient conditions exist, a specific
kind of crime is likely to occur in a certain type of location.
These predictions take the form of if-then rules with associated probabilities as in the following illustration:

> For Center of City
> if Weather includes Wet
> and Day is Friday
> and Time is Night
> then Problems will include inside bars
> (probability 0.9)

> For Center of City
> if Weather includes Dry
> if Weather includes Warm
> and Day is Friday
> and Time is Night
> then Problems areas will include outside
>   bars (probability 0.9)
> and Problems will include inside bars
>   (probability 0.4)

Overall, the set of rules generated by a series of neural analyses does not assume a simple linear relationship between ambient factors and crime but rather brings to light sets of circumstances under which specific types of crime are apt to occur, allowing law enforcement to allocate resources appropriately on an a priori rather than post-facto basis.

Just as an architect must have a blueprint for a large building, so too law enforcement officials must have a model of criminal activity as a basis for a policing strategy. Models help members of enforcement teams test their assumptions, identify what is important, predict what may be successful, allocate police resources effectively, and assess the match of theory to practice. When combined with geographic information systems, the crime maps that emerge from various modeling techniques provide a graphic way of communicating alternative crime-fighting strategies to citizens, city decision-makers, and members of the law enforcement community.

Summary

One of the advanced goals of crime analysts is the use of computerized crime mapping to model various aspects of crime. Since crime is a multifaceted phenomenon, knowing the most important variables helps to focus limited resources. Three operations are particularly useful in this goal: spatial situational and spatial historical analysis, multivariate pattern analysis, and spatial modeling.

Spatial situational analysis involves analyzing types of

crime by types of setting. For example, are convenience store robberies more likely to end in homicide? Spatial historical analysis involves studying the relationship of non-crime event histories to crime patterns. Events may include sporting events, concerts, festivals, and so on. Each type of event may be associated with particular types of crime.

Multivariate pattern analysis attempts to study crime in conjunction with other variables. These variables may include social, cultural, and economic variables, which also may be complex to define. Multivariate pattern analysis attempts to isolate the most important variables contributing to the pattern. Isolating the important variables allows police departments to focus limited resources on the leading causes of the crime pattern.

Spatial modeling refers to statistical techniques that operationalize the theories of crime in order to forecast it. Some of these techniques include structural equation modeling and neural network analysis. The prevailing theories of crime most often used in computerized crime analysis are "routine activities theory," "environmental theory," and "social disorganization theory." Crime analysts have developed a variety of mapping techniques that are used in conjunction with these theories. Most of these techniques are focused on identifying probable areas for locating an offender or a potential crime location.

Questions

1. Describe the concept of spatial situational analysis. Give an example of using this concept in police work.
2. Identify possible ways a police department can use spatial historical analysis.
3. Why would a police department use multivariate crime analysis?
4. In terms of crime mapping, what is spatial modeling?
5. What is a criminologic model?
6. Briefly describe the relationship between the following terms: spatial situational analysis, multivariate pattern analysis, and spatial modeling.

CHAPTER 5

Crime Mapping and Police Decision-Making

Mapping for Pattern Detection and Decision-Making

In order to effectively combat crime, police strategy since the 1970s has been shifting from reactive calls for service activity to proactive methods of identifying crime patterns and intervening in their causes. As GIS software has become more powerful and available, it has become an integral part of police strategy and decision-making process. Geographic information systems enable police commanders to see crime patterns in relation to their environment and visibly identify potentially troubling clusters of incidents. As we

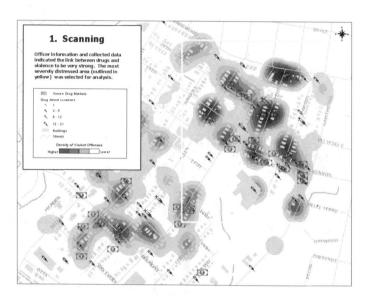

FIGURE 5.1 Scanning, the First Phase of the SARA Process. *Matthew White, Charlotte-Mecklenburg Police Department; used with permission.*

note in other sections of this book, the Compstat process as well as COP and POP rely heavily on GIS maps as part of the proactive approach to law enforcement.

One of the hazards of using GIS technologies is information overload. There may be so much data from different sources that information becomes lost in the background. A pin map with hundreds of dots is an example of information overload. As police departments progress beyond elementary pin mapping, pattern recognition and detection become an important use of mapping resources. Information may be infinite, but police resources are not. When a pattern is detected, it is important to decide where and how to focus resources as well to understand if the proposed solution to the problem actually worked.

The model currently used by many departments to identify crime problems and allocate police resources is SARA.[1] The SARA model was developed in the mid 1980s as part of the POP method of combating crime. It is a methodical, step-by-step process departments can use to address crime problems. In each of the four steps of the SARA process, computerized crime mapping can play an important supporting role.

Scanning

- In the scanning phase of SARA, departments attempt to identify the recurring problems concerning the police and the community. Crime mapping is useful for spotting potential crime trends in the form of clusters or hotspots. From the clusters and hotspots, particular problem areas may be selected for more in-depth investigation. In Figure 5.1, as part of the scanning process, analysts and officers in the Charlotte-Mecklenburg Police Department hypothesize that there is a connection between drug arrests and incidents of violence.

Analysis

- During the analysis phase, an attempt is made to understand the underlying causes associated with the problem. Computerized crime mapping allows the analyst to examine the problem in the context of other variables. For example, as we have noted before, there are demographic as well as sociological variables that may impact or contribute to crime clusters. Geographic information system technology allows the integration of information from other public agencies that may impact the problem. During this phase, departments may use techniques such as brainstorming to propose potential solutions to selected problem areas. In Figure 5.2, analysts incorporate home address data in an effort to understand the geographic dispersion of those purchasing drugs. In other words, "Where do the customers come from?"

Response

- The response phase builds on the scanning and analysis phase. In this phase the department proposes and applies techniques as well as resources to address the problem.

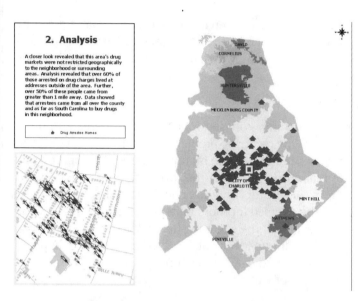

2. Analysis

A closer look revealed that this area's drug markets were not restricted geographically to the neighborhood or surrounding areas. Analysis revealed that over 60% of those arrested on drug charges lived at addresses outside of the area. Further, over 50% of these people came from greater than 1 mile away. Data showed that arrestees came from all over the county and as far as South Carolina to buy drugs in this neighborhood.

◆ Drug Arrestee Homes

FIGURE 5.2 Analysis, the Second Phase of the SARA Process. *Matthew White, Charlotte-Mecklenburg Police Department; used with permission.*

Computerized crime mapping in this phase may be used to model the possible responses to the problem. In Figures 4A.1 and 4A.2, the problem appears to be that drug customers living more than a mile from the sales sites have easy access to sellers from their vehicles. Essentially, there appears to be a "drive-in" or "drive-by" market. The hypothesis is that by focusing on interrupting the drug market, the incidents of violence will be reduced. In Figure 5.3 the response to the problem is to break up the rhythm of the street market by impeding traffic with barricades.

Assessment

• As part of the assessment phase, departments must determine whether their response to the problem has been measurably effective. Assessment data may be gathered from several sources ranging from incident reports, calls for service, arrests, and even citizen surveys. In Figure 5.4

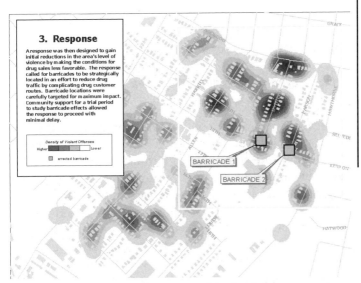

3. Response

A response was then designed to gain initial reductions in the area's level of violence by making the conditions for drug sales less favorable. The response called for barricades to be strategically located in an effort to reduce drug traffic by complicating drug customer routes. Barricade locations were carefully targeted for maximum impact. Community support for a trial period to study barricade effects allowed the response to proceed with minimal delay.

Density of Violent Offenses
Higher ▮▮▮▮▮ Lower

□ errected barricade

BARRICADE 1

BARRICADE 2

FIGURE 5.3 Response, the Third Phase of the SARA Process. *Matthew White, Charlotte-Mecklenburg Police Department; used with permission.*

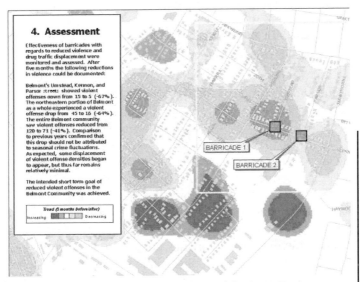

4. Assessment

Effectiveness of barricades with regards to reduced violence and drug traffic displacement were monitored and assessed. After five months the following reductions in violence could be documented:

Belmont's Umstead, Kennon, and Parson streets showed violent offenses down from 15 to 5 (-67%). The northeastern portion of Belmont as a whole experienced a violent offense drop from 45 to 16 (-64%). The entire Belmont community saw violent offenses reduced from 120 to 71 (-41%). Comparison to previous years confirmed that this drop should not be attributed to seasonal crime fluctuations. As expected, some displacement of violent offense densities began to appear, but thus far remains relatively minimal.

The intended short term goal of reduced violent offenses in the Belmont Community was achieved.

Trend (5 months before/after)
Increasing ▮▮▮▮▮ Decreasing

BARRICADE 1

BARRICADE 2

FIGURE 5.4 Assessment, the Fourth Phase of the SARA Process. *Matthew White, Charlotte-Mecklenburg Police Department; used with permission.*

the effectiveness of adding the barricades is determined by comparing the density of violent crimes to previous observation periods. Based on incident reports, the numbers of violent crimes in the target area were significantly reduced even when adjusted for seasonal variation in the crimes.

Because the SARA model is important to the POP model, there is a prestigious award for effective and innovative applications of the technique to crime problems. The Police Executive Research Forum presents the annual Herman Goldstein Award[2] to selected police departments in the United States or abroad. One of the major criteria for the award is that projects must achieve measurable results in reducing crime or public disorder problems. As part of the submission process, applicants must identify a problem and address each of the four parts of the SARA model. Since 1999 many of the annual winners of the Herman Goldstein award have used some aspect of computerized crime mapping in conjunction with the SARA process.

Mapping Time Series and Spatial Displacements

As useful as crime mapping is in locating crime hot spots, strategic law enforcement planning requires a long-term overview of trends based on the analysis of time series. Time-series analysis of crime throws light on crime trends by jurisdiction and has long been a statistical tool of crime analysts (Bennett 1991). For instance, analysts in Washington DC are using GIS to study the spatial patterns of elevated blood lead levels in children, in a project sponsored by the national Crime Mapping Research Center. Spatial analysis reveals characteristics such as toxic release over time and by location. Results of this study inform enforcement and help in abatement and prevention efforts.[3] To take a second simple illustration, seven daily time-of-day maps for a particular crime such as domestic disturbances, one for each day of the week, can aid policy in allocating resources to this type of crime, both spatially and temporally.

One method of analyzing crime time series is through using a series of isopleth maps. Isopleth maps create contour lines of crime density much as topographical maps create contour lines based on elevation. Such maps are more related to crime than are choropleth (shaded) maps based on arbitrary political boundaries such as census tracts or zip codes. The contours created with isopleth maps can be color-coded according to degree of crime intensity. By creating a series of such isopleth maps over time, law enforcement officials can spot where there have been significant increases in certain types of crime and where these increases have occurred (LeBeau 1997). The series of maps can even be made into an animation so that the user may view the time series as a miniature "movie," as does Crime-Point 2002 AutoTheft software, which is designed to help police spot trends in vehicular larceny.[4]

Time-series crime mapping can be helpful in individual cases in addition to understanding broad crime patterns. Time series analysis across related crimes can also be a tool for uncovering criminals whose activities fall into common patterns of crime evolution. For instance, it has been found that rapists often start their careers with lesser crimes, such as indecent exposure, being a "peeping tom," and break-ins. By tracing the spatial evolution of such "precursor crimes" over time, police can develop suspect databases for current target crimes like rape.

Spatial displacement refers to the movement of criminals from one location to another in response to some police enforcement action. Law enforcement officials worry about spatial displacement because their goal is to reduce overall crime levels, not just shift crime from one area to another in an endless chase after hotspots. Spatial displacement is closely linked to six other types of displacement noted by Barnes (1995):

• Criminals shift from more-policed areas to less-policed areas (spatial displacement).

- Criminals shift from protected targets to vulnerable targets (target displacement).
- Criminals shift from risky time of day to less risky (temporal displacement).
- Criminals shift to avoid security systems (tactical displacement).
- Criminals shift from types of crime with low reward/risk ratios to types of crime with high reward/risk ratios (crime-type displacement)
- New offenders enter areas vacated by experienced criminals (perpetrator displacement).

Of the six types of displacement, data are most readily available for spatial displacement, and consequently spatial displacement is the easiest to map. Still, there are various reasons why mapping spatial displacement encounters methodological problems (Weisburd and Green 1995). When crime is rising, police enforcement may only cause crime to increase at a slower rate, yet the analyst may have difficulty being assured that enforcement rather than some other reason (e.g., more opportunities in other areas) is the critical cause. When crime is high, temporal variations in crime may be larger than and may wash out statistically any effect of police enforcement. Nonetheless, crime mapping of apparent spatial displacements at least provides working theories about the effects of police enforcement actions, theories that can be tested in the course of debriefing arrestees.

Mapping of spatial displacements may also refer to tracking the activities of specific criminals or groups of criminals. Such maps must be accurate in order to withstand challenge in criminal court. One GIS manager noted, "I too am aware of savvy defense lawyers that have discredited map compositions and calculations created by police and prosecutors simply because they could not state (because they did not know) the accuracy of the map source data" (Norton 2001). Thus when Montgomery County, Maryland, police use crime mapping to enforce additional penalties for crimes committed within predetermined distances from school boundaries, for instance, they are careful to actually compute the distances from the property line of schools and not merely from the centroid of the property (Sweeney 2001). Another jurisdiction prints the spatial accuracy level of the data on any maps it distributes (e.g. $+\backslash -2.5$ feet) and the map is signed by a city-licensed surveyor (Norton 2001).

Integrating Interagency Data

The subject of information sharing between law enforcement and other agencies has grown in importance since the tragic events of September 11, 2001, which have raised important issues about interagency cooperation and data sharing. The ecological theory of crime proposes that there are unique characteristics about the places where crime occurs. Understanding the environment in order to intervene in crime or comprehend its origins requires a complex set of data such that one agency could not possibly gather. In order to obtain various types of data, many police departments are exploring how to share data with other public agencies. Integration is the term frequently used to describe applying technological solutions to information management and sharing data among government agencies. Sharing data among agencies provides several advantages for participating agencies. One of the major advantages is that shared information is less expensive. In economic terms, the agency receiving the data only incurs the cost of the transfer and not the cost of creating the data. For example, in order to use computerized crime-mapping software effectively, police departments need accurate street center-line data to create a base map. If these data were not provided by the city planning department, another agency, or a commercial source, then police departments would have to devote considerable resources to creating and maintaining the map. Another advantage to sharing, besides cost, is the ability to access a diverse selection of data types collected by various public agencies.

One of the key elements discussed in the COP and POP section is using various types of information as an aid for addressing community problems. Addressing community concerns may require a range of local demographic and sociological information not readily available through census resources. Suppose, for example, a community is concerned with the rowdy behavior of certain teenagers after the school day. Mapping both the location and time of the rowdy behavior is easy enough. A community officer may want to map the incidents in relation to the surrounding area, looking for a migration pattern or a particular hotspot. Addressing the roots of the problem in order to intervene may also require a broader understanding of demographics of the neighborhood. Other important information to map may include city recreation or other programs that are available as an option for channeling rowdy behavior. In other words, intervening in the problem of rowdy behavior requires different types of data that police departments do not ordinarily collect for themselves.

The National Performance Review in its report on crime mapping and data-driven management noted an example of using data integration to intervene in crime in the Charlotte-Mecklenburg Police Department in North Carolina:

> The way it works is this. The Charlotte-Mecklenburg Police Department intervenes in crime and social disorder problems by gathering information from any and all city agencies to determine the most reliable remedy for a given problem. Information integration is the key. It is the basis for the department's analysis of a given situation and for a preventive, proactive approach that is fueled by the linking of databases from agencies in the city, county, or surrounding jurisdictions. By compiling information from as many sources as possible, officers and analysts are able to increase their understanding of the problem they may be facing.

Integrating Interagency Data

Data sharing between the police and other public agencies provides the opportunity to obtain information of greater importance than the individual pieces of data. However, integrating diverse types of data requires a certain level of technological skill and an organizational commitment to seek new sources of data as well as share it. In addition, administrative tools like cooperative agreements and memorandums of understanding aid the data integration process, creating a framework for sharing as well as outlining an agency's responsibilities within the integration process.

Sharing data between agencies requires both compatible technology and information architecture. Presently there are no national mandates for any particular technology design, and many information systems in the law enforcement community began as unique "stand-alone" systems. Compatibility for data sharing in today's computing environment begins with using the same operating system platform. It also means that agencies must have a method of communicating with each other either through intranets or the Internet itself.[5] The improved technology and proliferation of personal computers as well as the arrival of the Internet have made it easier to exchange data between agencies. However, just having compatible technology is not synonymous with sharing data.

Another technological component affecting data sharing is the software used to collect and process data. In police departments this usually means the records management system and the computer aided dispatch system, which can be tied to the components of GIS, enhancing the capability of police departments to integrate data. Using GIS, even data from other agencies can be combined with police data, then mapped. Integrated data provide a richer contextual environment for analysis than just arrest and calls-for-service data.

For many years police departments have shared data with other law enforcement agencies through various crime reports and criminal history databases. In order to gain the benefits of interagency integration, sharing cannot be a one-way street. Police departments must be willing not only to share with each other but with other public agencies as well. Data sharing has two organizational components, horizontal sharing and vertical sharing. Horizontal sharing occurs between agencies at the same level of government, as, for example, sharing data between a police department and a city public housing office. Vertical sharing, on the other hand, is sharing information between different levels of government such as between a city police department and the federal government. Data sharing is aided by using administrative tools like cooperative agreements and memorandums of understanding.[6] In their simplest form, these tools are used among agencies to specify what data will be shared and with whom.

Federal Data-Sharing Initiatives

One of the reasons for using crime mapping is to take advantage of its analytical power to solve community-wide problems and intervene in crime. However, this is only possible if community agencies and police departments are sharing their data. One of the newer initiatives of the Department of Justice is the Community Mapping Planning and Analysis for Safety Strategies, a program designed to analyze leading indicators of crime in a community using GIS and other technologies. In order to collect the appropriate indicators of crime, this program will facilitate data sharing between community agencies (Department of Justice 2002). At the time of this book's writing, Milwaukee, Wisconsin, and Seattle, Washington, were both actively participating with the Department of Justice as program sites.[7]

Another example of multiagency collaboration is the Strategic Approaches To Community Safety Initiative (SACSI), a program developed by the Department of Justice to promote multiagency collaboration to reduce crime as well as use GIS technologies to seek data-driven solutions to local problems. The SACSI program has three aims (Coleman et al. 1999):

• Bring together various communities and groups to address a major crime problem.

- Integrate the knowledge of front-line officers and researchers to create specific responses to crime.
- Adapt the strategy in response to information analysis.

In order to implement the SACSI program, the CMRC is aiding five pilot cities to develop a newer type of information system that is integrated, user friendly, interagency, and Internet based. These are important characteristics if the communities employing SACSI expect to use the approach to address a variety of crime problems. This newer information system is called the Community Safety Information System and it will allow the participating agencies to merge their various datasets and analyze new relationships found in the merger (Coleman et al. 1999). With information provided by an integrated data-sharing approach, police departments and their communities will be in a better position to strategically intervene in major crime problems.

Summary

Computerized crime mapping is becoming indispensable for police managers. In order to identify and focus on specific problems, police departments are now using SARA a four-step process. Geographic information system technology is used in each step of this process.

Computerized crime mapping is also used to map time-series data and spatial displacement of crime. Time-series data allow police management to view crime as it evolves over time. Time-series applications can vary from a period of hours to even years. One cutting-edge method of visualizing time-series data is to use animation techniques.

The spatial displacement of crime is the movement of criminal activity from one location to another in response to police enforcement activity. Spatial displacement is a concern for any police department because shifting crime problems is not the same as solving them.

In order to realize the full potential of computerized crime mapping, police departments are beginning to share data with each other as well as other agencies. Sharing data has many benefits for an agency. The main benefit is that shared data is less expensive than creating data, but data sharing also brings information on additional crime factors to bear on crime analysis using GIS.

Presently several initiatives are being funded by the Department of Justice to encourage data sharing between police and other agencies. Two pilot programs are SACSI and Community Mapping Planning and Analysis for Safety Strategies. Each of these programs focuses on creating an interagency, collaborative environment to share data on selected community indicators.

Questions

1. Explain the four components of the SARA model by which police departments may identify crime problems and allocate police resources. Why is crime mapping relevant to each of the four components?
2. Why may isopleth maps be more related to crime patterns than choropleth (shaded) maps?
3. What is "spatial displacement"? Explain its six types.
4. Give three different reasons why police agencies may wish to share data with other agencies.
5. Explain the difference between vertical data sharing as opposed to horizontal data sharing.
6. What is SACSI?

CHAPTER 6

Crime Mapping for City Police Chiefs and County Sheriffs

How Crime Mapping Enhances Effectiveness

Crime mapping enhances effectiveness at all levels. Detectives can use crime mapping to track the patterns of serial criminals. The patrol officer can be more alert to locations of recent crime activity. Precinct chiefs can assign resources more wisely. Department heads can observe trends and engage in strategic planning on a more informed basis. Moreover, crime mapping provides an effective tool for community policing, for communicating with the media, and as a basis for policy and funding discussions in city councils and county boards. For instance, crime mapping can be used effectively to compare survey-reported fear of crime with actual crime by city district, allowing citizens and decision-makers alike to understand that public perception is not always factual reality (Velasco and Boba 2000b).

Consider the mapping of stolen vehicle recovery locations as an illustration of how crime mapping enhances effectiveness. Knowing where stolen vehicles are found can be more important than knowing where they are stolen from because criminals often leave stolen vehicles near where they are stripped down for parts—near chop shops. Baltimore County, for instance, used crime mapping to show where stolen vehicles were recovered, demonstrating that many stolen in the suburbs were recovered in Baltimore City. Chop shops discovered by police were also mapped, showing them to be located in the same areas. This reinforced the strategy of seeking new chop shops when police uncover concentrations of stolen vehicle recoveries in the same general area (Crime Mapping Research Center 2001).

As another example, crime mapping can overlay patterns of drug trafficking on a map of the location of public pay phones. This information can allow police to increase patrols in these areas or even to arrange for the removal of phones associated with drug transactions. Likewise, as Ratcliffe and McCullagh (1998) have shown, GIS can dramatically improve the ability of police to identify repeat crimes and thus to make appropriate changes in policing strategy. The ways in which crime mapping can enhance law enforcement effectiveness are almost too numerous to mention, but here are a few more examples taken from recent practice.

- The National Guard Bureau Counterdrug Directorate created in 1993 a Digital Mapping Initiative that provides free computer-generated maps to hundreds of law enforcement agencies throughout the country with over 100,000 mapping products. The utility of these maps in fighting drug crime is attested by the high volume of repeat agency business (Thomas 1999).
- The Sacramento Police Department was the first law enforce-

ment agency in the country to give citizens access to interactive crime mapping via the Internet. Citizens can view crime trends for any three months by area, crime type, and other variables.[1]

- The Tempe (AZ) Police Department puts crime maps and crime data on the Internet to "provide timely information with nearly instantaneous updates and conserve time and resources by reducing mailings and virtually eliminating printing and duplicating costs" (Boba 1999). This also allows citizen phone calls on neighborhood safety issues to be referred to the Internet, lessening staff work and allowing citizens to make their own assessments.[2]

- Baltimore police have found that crime analyses are conducted in one-sixth the time since the advent of automated crime mapping (Kelly 1999).

- Overland Park (KS) Police produce 3-foot by 4-foot crime maps for use in the courtroom by prosecutors, garnering numerous comments about their effectiveness with juries (Tallman, Wernicke, and May 1999).

- Knoxville (TN) police used crime mapping in a rape case by developing a suspect database by overlaying a map of residences of sex offenders, parolees, and juvenile habitual offenders on top of a map of rape offenses. Later, victims were able to identify the offender from the suspect database. Police stated that "without the spatial analysis of the offender databases layered on top of the crime scene map, the offender information would not have been readily known" (Hubbs 1998).

- Correction officers in Orleans Parish (LA) are using crime mapping to track jail inmates with respect to gang affiliations.[3]

- The Wisconsin Department of Corrections uses GIS to create density maps of locations of parolees for purposes of prioritizing areas in need of increased neighborhood supervision and focusing on community-based corrections in dealing with businesses, neighbors, and local officials rather than focusing narrowly on offenders (Mixdorf 1999).

- The Monmouth County (NJ) Prosecutor's Office uses crime mapping to map school zones for both Megan's Law notifications and determinations of "drug-free school zones" (Hartman 2001).

- County (MD) Police Dept uses crime mapping to enforce additional penalties for crimes committed within predetermined distances from school boundaries (Sweeney 2001).

- Polk County (IA) public safety officials used GIS to map how far existing tornado sirens reached, thereby revealing gaps in coverage enabling reconfiguration of the warning system (Mumm 2001).
- The Community Justice Project of the Center of Alternative Sentencing and Employment Services in New York City used crime mapping to show that the allocation of corrections funding was not consistent with what would be expected on the basis of proportion of males sentenced to prison by neighborhood, correctional facility admissions by block, and inmate residences (Cadora and Clear 1999). Similar strategic resource planning using crime mapping has been implemented by the Delaware Department of Corrections (Harris 1999).
- Aurora (CO) police used crime mapping to show that burglaries clustered geographically. This, in turn, enabled them to distribute information in the areas thus identified, leading almost immediately to the identification and apprehension of a suspect, whose residence turned out to be at the center of the cluster that had been mapped (Brown, Lawless, Lu, and Rogers 1998).
- The San Diego Police Department has used crime mapping to compare the distribution of property crime to streetlight illumination for purposes of evaluating investment in the latter.
- A police department critical incident manager can employ three-dimensional mapping to "fly" through a building that is the location of a hostage situation, enabling more realistic planning for SWAT teams.
- In Washington/Baltimore's High Intensity Drug Trafficking Area (HIDTA) region, the Evaluation and Crime Mapping Unit maintains the COMETS database on drug transactions, firearms trafficking, and money laundering based on data obtained by taking a random sample of investigations and following up with interviews. The database allows crime mappers to depict changes in drug, firearms, and "dirty money" traffickers' communications and transactions. Crime mapping allows HIDTA (2001) to identify specific high-traffic drug areas by address, correlating this over time with enforcement initiatives for the purpose of assessing their effectiveness.
- MapInfo, a leading GIS package, played an important role in recovery efforts for TWA Flight 800 off Long Island in 1996,

mapping debris on the sea floor, and helping analyze whether the disaster was terrorism or an accident (Kelly 1999).

- New York City police and emergency services benefited after the September 11, 2001, terrorist attack on the World Trade Center by using GIS software to map the rubble pile for purposes of securing the perimeter, clearing routes for heavy equipment, assigning areas for crane placement, locating positions for support services, and assigning areas of responsibility for search and excavation teams (Howard 2002). As a result of September 11, "responder-friendly" GIS software was developed and ready for the Olympic Winter Games a few months later should a terrorist attack have happened there.

Many more examples of the effectiveness of GIS in law enforcement may be found in *Crime Mapping Case Studies*, edited by Nancy Lavigne and Julie Wartell (2000) for the Police Forum. This anthology illustrates through specific examples how crime mapping was effective in better allocating police patrols to deal with a pattern of residential break-ins, in implementing a drug crackdown, in police redistricting, in carrying out neighborhood watch functions, in tracking down a serial sex crime suspect, in disproving a criminal's alibi through cell-phone mapping, in enforcing compliance with a sex offender registration program, in the analysis of gun violence, and in optimizing closed-circuit television use for surveillance purposes.

Crime mapping enables decision-makers access to pertinent, graphic information on variables that previously were often out of reach. For instance, tactical and strategy sessions may now request information "on the fly" about the proximity of crimes to schools, establishments serving alcoholic beverages, hazardous materials storage locations, recreation areas, or other community features as well as the relation of crimes to time of day, day of week, or even weather patterns. District attorneys' offices may benefit from use of high-resolution GIS maps in forensic cartography to display the relation of weapons or other objects to each other or to victims. Even patrol officers benefit. When a crime incident occurs at a school, for example, the San Diego Police Department can quickly produce and transmit to patrol officers a map of the layout of a school and its adjacent area.

New York's Compstat System

Compstat is a management system for law enforcement that centers on holding police precinct commanders accountable for crime in their areas, reviewed in weekly city-wide meetings that focus on crime maps and crime data trends.[4] Patterns identified through crime mapping are followed up by commanders, who seek to fashion a comprehensive response involving community groups and ongoing assessment, using impact measures to evaluate progress toward crime reduction. Compstat was a key tool in the dramatic reduction of crime in New York City in the 1990s and has since been copied by numerous other jurisdictions (e.g., by the Wisconsin Department of Corrections [Mixdorf 1999]). Compstat has also been popularized nationally in fictional form (using real GIS software) in the television show, *The District*, in which Chief Mansion relies extensively on Ella Farmer, his director of crime analysis and her GIS-based reports, modeled after the New York system (Theodore 2001).

Introduced as a new form of crime control strategy meeting in 1994 by Howard Safar, New York City's Police Commissioner, Compstat allows police to track crime incidents almost in real time. Data tracked include information on the crime incident, victim information, time of day of the incident, and other variables that result in computer-generated maps illustrating city-wide crime trends used to identify trouble spots and then used to target resources to deal with crime on a strategic basis. Although crime mapping had been used by many jurisdictions, the Compstat system was a pioneer in creating a management process around GIS technology. Compstat brings together New

York's 76 precinct commanders as well as top departmental managers. These officials review crime data, partly by using crime maps, and analyze ways to reduce crime trends that are spotted. Precinct commanders are expected to report on steps they have taken to address specific crime developments and, indeed, the purpose of Compstat centers on holding precinct commanders accountable, but also through results-oriented interactive management, giving commanders increased discretion as to just how resources at their command are utilized. The Compstat process involves continuous monitoring of results to make accountability an ongoing process.

Weekly or biweekly from 7:00 to 10:00 a.m., New York City police leadership and precinct commanders meet in a large conference room, seated at tables near a large-screen projection system capable of displaying maps and charts related to topics under discussion. Precincts under review rotate on a monthly schedule. In a typical discussion, a commander may take note of a series of break-ins in his or her precinct, and they may be questioned about whether this is related to robbery parolees residing in the precinct. Mapping staffs are capable of creating on the fly precinct maps that display a very wide variety of types of crime locations, hotspots, and related information. Under the Compstat process, staff will instantly display a map of parolee addresses to provide data on the subject. That is, the Compstat process is a data-guided accountability-centered approach to management by results, one in which crime mapping plays a central role as an aid to policy and tactical discussions and decisions.

Compstat is often summarized in terms of four principles: (1) "Accurate and timely intelligence" allows law enforcement officials from the beat officer to the commissioner of police to know immediately what types of crimes have been committed where, how, and by whom; (2) "effective tactics" involve cross-agency and even cross-jurisdiction cooperation as well as community outreach operations; (3) "rapid deployment of personnel and resources" creates an immediate, focused response to crime problems; (4) "relentless follow-up and assessment" ensures that targets are met and desired results are achieved.

One further aspect of the Compstat management process extends community policing by inviting school officials, neighborhood groups, local business leaders, and other community representatives to attend Compstat meetings. Crime patterns that cross precinct lines are easily spotted, providing the information needed for community groups to work together on common interests as well as for precinct commanders to collaborate on joint enforcement efforts.

Philadelphia's Crimestat System

Philadelphia must field over three million 911 emergency calls a year. Potentially responding to these calls, directly or in a support role, are some 7,000 police officers and some 1,000 civilian support staff. Among these is a GIS unit composed of three civilian staff and one police officer.[5] The GIS unit participates actively in the Crimestat process, which involves New York City-like meetings on a rotating weekly schedule with two to three divisions the focus of each week's session. Maps produced for these oversight, planning, and accountability meetings include ones on types of crime (e.g., homicides, rapes, property crimes, drug offenses) and on special topics as needed (e.g., gunshot incident density, time-of-day incident patterns).

The Philadelphia Police Department implemented a version of Compstat in 1998 under Philadelphia Police Commissioner John F. Timoney, a former New York City officer instrumental in creating Compstat in New York.[6] Philadelphia's Crime Analysis and Mapping Unit (CAMU), established in September 1997 with a Local Law Enforcement Block Grant, produces up to 2,000 maps weekly. The CAMU GIS staff breaks down crime by type, weapon, time of day, day of week, residential/commercial location, and other variables. By comparing current crime maps with those of previous months, precinct commanders can both assess the effectiveness of past anti-crime strategies and plan new ones. As in New York, Crimestat statistical information is used as the basis for weekly 3-hour meetings of the police commissioner and top law enforcement management.

Since 1997, data for Crimestat have come from Philadelphia's Incident Reporting System computer program, which, in turn, is based on incident reports filed by police officers. These incident reports are prepared using categories and procedures defined by the federally mandated Uniform Crime Reporting (UCR) system. After a 5-day period used for data verification and review, Incident Reporting System data is fed into the Crimestat process and is used in its associated management reviews and strategic planning processes. A Quality Assurance Bureau also independently audits the quality of Crimestat data.

As in New York, CAMU maps are projected onto a large screen in the front of the Crimestat meeting room, providing a backdrop as the police commissioner, backed up by aides, questions district commanders about what map hotspots reveal. Commanders must report on progress on issues identified in prior Crimestat meetings, explain trends in crime and quality of life offenses, and describe their tactical plans for addressing new situations.

Crimestat meetings can be intimidating for district commanders, who must justify decisions in their jusrisdictions. Crimestat meetings are attended not only by the police commissioner, but also by his five deputy commissioners, the chiefs of the Patrol, Training, Special Operations, and Quality Assurance Bureaus. Crimestat meetings are also attended by the commanders of the Department's specialized and support units such as Highway Patrol, Major Crimes, Special Victims, Homicide, and Internal Affairs, as well as representatives of the suburban, transit, and local university police departments. Parole and probation officers and representatives from the district attorney's office and other city agencies also regularly attend, as do representatives of the media. This pattern of broad public attention intensifies accountability by district commanders but also forges city-wide partnerships to fight crime in Philadelphia.

In Philadelphia, two of the six Patrol Bureau Divisions and their corresponding Detective Bureau Divisions are the focus of a Crimestat meeting each week for a period of three weeks. Every fourth week, the meeting focuses on specialized units such as SWAT, Canine, Mounted, Aviation, Bomb Disposal, Environmental Response, Marine, and Accident Investigation. Thus a commander in a given district can be expected to have his district the subject of Crimestat focus about once a month. Because the maps take about a week to prepare, Crimestat meeting data are about a week old, allowing commanders to prepare for their questioning at an upcoming meeting. The result is intensive research and analysis of crime trends, deployment strategies, disposition of offenders, and other data as the accountable officers seek to assure their strategic planning has not overlooked appropriate responses and left their units open to criticism at Crimestat meetings.

Crimestat was an immediate success, to which crime mapping was critical. As areas of high crime density were identified, police resources were reallocated more efficiently for purposes of crime response. Crime maps of stolen car recovery locations helped Philadelphia police track down and bust chop shops.

As the utility of crime maps became well known within the Philadelphia Police Department, a need arose to decentralize the process of producing maps so that this was no longer the sole province of the central GIS unit but rather became a routine operation of the district offices. District-level crime mapping allows district commanders to review crime trends in real time, adjusting the deployment of law enforcement personnel accordingly. Daily district-level analysis of neighborhood crime trends gives district commanders the ability to deploy their resources as they judge to be most effective, just as Crimestat enables the same thing for the police commissioner on a city-wide basis. District offices were able to install ESRI's MapObjects Professional desktop software and were able to create incident query forms using ESRI's built-in programming language (Visual Basic). Using these forms, police officers can enter information on the type of map wanted, submit the form, and receive a map portraying the requested type of incidents. Moreover, using another ESRI product, MapObjects IMS, requested maps can be distributed via secure Internet to any number of people, sending timely maps out to street-level patrol officers. For instance, patrol officers can get a map or chart of all incidents at a given address or of types of crimes occurring on a given street between the hours of midnight and 6 a.m.

Numerous other cities have implemented Compstat- and Crimestat-like operations:

* Chicago Police established the Information Collection for Automated Mapping system for distribution of crime maps to patrol officers engaged in community policing. Such maps were credited with helping mobilize community-based neighborhood surveillance and tips leading to arrests and reduction in crime.
* Delaware police created the Delaware Real Time Crime Reporting system based on Intergraph GeoMedia software.
* The San Diego Police Department pioneered SARA, which, starting in 1989, used crime maps and crime data as part of a problem-solving approach to police decision-making.

By the start of the twenty-first century, Compstat-type law enforcement planning, resting in no small part on geospatial analysis and computer mapping, was quickly becoming the recommended method of organizing policy operations.

Regional Approaches to Crime Mapping

Within the law enforcement community, it has been noted that crime does not stop at jurisdiction lines. Regional approaches to crime mapping have several advantages to offer. One of the advantages is the ability to see beyond the jurisdiction level to monitor emerging trends that may migrate across boundaries. Regional mapping then serves as an early warning system and forum for police cooperation. Another advantage is the ability to pool resources, since establishing GIS for crime analysis requires a significant investment of resources in terms of hardware, software, and training. With the advantages of a centralized approach, regional crime mapping helps smaller jurisdictions acquire the benefits of computerized crime mapping. The term "regional" has no precise definition, and the idea of crossing jurisdictional boundaries has been discussed under several terms. In fact, the authors interviewed a police sergeant in Seattle who defined a region in the following manner, making the definition of region dependent on the nature of the crime:

> I think you really need to look at the span, the span of movement of your average criminal to determine the size, the breadth that you might need to reach to get adequate coverage regionally. (Garson and Vann 2001: 24)

Cooperation between two or more law enforcement agencies has been discussed in the literature as interjurisdictional or multijurisdictional efforts. Recently the term cross-boundary crime mapping (CBCM) has been introduced to the crime-mapping vocabulary to describe two or more departments cooperating together on a sustained and continuous basis (Eck 2002).

Despite the variety of terms, any cooperative crime mapping between jurisdictions must be centered on commonly accepted goals (Greenwald 2000). Police departments operate within the sphere of public administration, so establishing a multi-jurisdictional crime-mapping effort is generally a product of at least three elements: support from the political or administrative leadership, a framework in which to operate, and technical compatibility among the participants. Support from political and administrative leadership usually involves oversight and vision as well as access to funding. Leadership support is a critical success factor for the acceptance as well as the continued maintenance of new technology initiatives.

Frameworks provide the operating rules for jurisdictions to exchange and analyze data. Examples of frameworks include memorandums of understanding, cooperative agreements, and even regional authorities. Memorandums of understanding and cooperative agreements are administrative tools similar to contracts in the commercial world. Participating parties, like police jurisdictions, sign them voluntarily and agree to abide by the covenants of the particular contract. Another type of framework is the regional authority that may facilitate all three aspects of a multi-jurisdictional crime-mapping effort. A regional authority may provide the leadership, the operating framework, and the technical compatibility for the participating members, essentially relieving them of the major burdens of the effort (Garson and Vann 2001; LaVigne and Wartell 2001).

Of the three elements, technical compatibility is probably the easiest to achieve since it usually involves jurisdictions using compatible DBMS file formats and computer-operating systems. Most commercial DBMS packages have a variety of choices for the output file formats such as comma and space separation as well as text formatting. GIS software such as ArcView will import files from MapInfo.

Cross-Boundary Crime Mapping

Cross-boundary crime mapping is an emerging approach to crime mapping that is initially defined as a relationship between two law enforcement agencies. Eck (2002) further defines CBCM by developing criteria for the concept. Data meeting the CBCM criteria are event-level data exchanged on a recurring basis that include information about the location of the event. One-time cooperative events between agencies like sporting or other special events are excluded from this definition (Eck 2002).

There are five factors that are conducive to establishing effective CBCM: actions, patterns, data, administration, and access (Eck, 2002).

- Actions—the agreed-upon efforts of the two or more agencies to address the problem.
- Patterns—are there interjurisdictional crime patterns?
- Data—do the cooperating agencies share similar data formats as well as reporting procedures?
- Administration—the cooperating agencies must agree on the timeliness of the data transfer as well as its governance.
- Access—the cooperating agencies must understand and agree on the rules of public dissemination and privacy.

Technological Approaches to Regional Crime Mapping

Some efforts at creating a regional approach to crime analysis are technology based. The technology-based programs share a common goal of allowing the user to look beyond their jurisdiction to detect migrating patterns of crime or patterns split by a jurisdictional boundary. Two unique and different approaches using technology are the Statewide Crime Analysis and Mapping Program (SCAMP) and the Regional Crime Analysis GIS program (RCAGIS). The SCAMP initiative is a solution to the shortage of crime analysts in small jurisdictions in Massachusetts. It involves centrally analyzing standard data submitted by departments and making it available to them through a secure website. RCAGIS, on the other hand, is a collection of software applications designed for local analysis. Users install RCAGIS on their local machine and pay a small licensing fee for using ESRI's MapObjects.

SCAMP is the abbreviation for the Statewide Crime Analysis and Mapping Program of the Massachusetts State Police. The SCAMP program was developed to provide crime mapping and analysis based on the capabilities of Massachusetts's smaller police jurisdictions. The Statistical Analysis Center of the Massachusetts Executive Office of Public Safety determined that in jurisdictions of 50,000 people and under, fewer than 20% of them were trained either in crime analysis or GIS. Furthermore, faced with typical constraints on public budgets, there was little likelihood of adding significant numbers of personnel just to do crime analysis (Bibel 2000).

SCAMP is designed to centrally analyze crime data submitted by jurisdictions. In order to standardize data collection, SCAMP uses a modified version of the National Incident Based Reporting Systems (NIBRS) format, collects significant incident level data yet lacks an address field for the incident. In order to map incident-level data, the Massachusetts Crime Reporting Unit added address fields to the NIBRS format along with latitude and longitude. When SCAMP reaches its full implementation level, participating agencies will be able to securely access maps driven by the NIBRS data that they and other departments have submitted. Additionally, upon its full implementation SCAMP will offer a standard set of analysis tools that includes buffering of incidents and their relationship to municipal boundaries along with demographic variables for an area based on census information.

Regional Crime Analysis GIS was developed by the Department of Justice using ESRI's MapObjects programming tools. The purpose of RCAGIS is to provide a standard set of analysis and mapping tools for law enforcement agencies to "see" beyond their jurisdictional boundaries along with generating standard automated reports. RCAGIS developed from an earlier initiative known as the Regional Crime Analysis System, which began in Maryland as a response to a string of related crimes occurring across several jurisdictions including the District of Columbia. It standardized the entry of incident information into databases so files became easier to share among the participating members.

The RCAGIS approach added two additional elements to effectively sharing database files. It added standardized analysis tools so that jurisdictions using the program would not only be able to share crime data, they would be able to analyze it as well. And it added automated reporting to turn the data into useful information. As previously noted, placing incidents on a map is an important start to crime analysis, but it is only a start. Analyzing and communicating information based on the data are equally important. For the analysis engine, RCAGIS uses CrimeStat, a spatial analysis program developed by Dr. Ned Levine and provided as shareware by the Department of Justice. The reporting tool uses Seagate Software's Crystal Reports to provided standard reports for each level of user from officer to analyst as well as command leadership.

The regional approach to crime mapping is multifaceted. Presently there is no "one size fits all" model for regional crime mapping. Each of the operating regional initiatives in the country has developed based on the unique requirements of their agencies. Many of the earliest initiatives began through the personal collaboration of individual crime analysts. As computerized crime mapping has matured, so have the approaches to regional crime mapping. New technological approaches like RCAGIS as well as comprehensive programs like COMPASS and SACSI are now available to guide communities seeking integrated, regional approaches to combating crime with data-driven initiatives.

Summary

Computerized crime mapping has become integral to developing enforcement strategies and monitoring police effectiveness. Many case studies published in police literature have highlighted how GIS has aided the law enforcement community in areas other than crime mapping. The cities of New York and Philadelphia were pioneers in applying computerized crime mapping to police operations.

The CBS television show, *The District,* is based on New York City's Compstat model. Compstat, however, is not crime mapping; it is a management system that holds police captains accountable for solving crime in their district. Crime mapping is one of the tools Compstat uses to spot crime trends and develop enforcement strategies. The Compstat approach is summarized by four principles:

1. Accurate and timely intelligence
2. Effective tactics
3. Rapid deployment of personnel and resources
4. Relentless follow-up and assessment

Likewise, Philadelphia uses a similar approach called Crimestat. The Crimestat approach to management closely resembles New York's Compstat. Philadelphia Police Commissioner John F. Timoney, a former New York City officer, was instrumental in establishing Crimestat in that city.

One of the oldest "truths" in policing is that crime does not stop at the jurisdiction border. With increased mobility, police and sheriff's departments are exploring the regional applications of crime mapping. Regional applications require cooperation as well as structure for collecting, analyzing, and sharing crime data. Agencies working on regional approaches use memorandums of agreement as a tool to facilitate the flow of data between them.

Questions

1. Give some examples of how crime mapping can enhance the effectiveness of a police department.
2. What are the four principles of the COMPSTAT program?
3. How are New York's COMPSTAT program and Philadelphia's CRIMESTAT program similar?
4. Give one reason for police departments and other law enforcement agencies to cooperate regionally.
5. What are some administrative tools used to facilitate regional cooperation?
6. What are some technological approaches to achieving regional cooperation?

CHAPTER 7

Public Concerns with Crime Mapping

Crime Databases and Individual Privacy

In July 1999 the CMRC hosted a 2-day Crime Mapping and Data Confidentiality Roundtable[1] to generate discussion and initial guidance on issues of confidentiality, data sharing, and related security issues pertaining to crime mapping. Participants included representatives from law enforcement, the research community, the legal profession, the GIS field, victim advocacy, and the media. The product of this meeting was a research report, *Privacy in the Information Age: A Guide for Sharing Crime Maps and Spatial Data Series,* by Julie Wartell and J. Thomas McEwen (2001).

The conference participants noted that crime does not stop at jurisdictional boundaries and that the power of GIS to identify problem areas and target scarce resources more efficiently in law enforcement rests on data-sharing capabilities within and among agencies and organizations, involving greater access by more persons to vast amounts of data. The increasing use of Internet maps and data servers for crime mapping can increase access exponentially. Widespread access, in turn, raises profound issues of individual privacy and data confidentiality, particularly as the existence of crime-mapping databases has elicited demand for information access not only from law enforcement personnel but also from community groups, businesses, and even individuals looking for crime-related information.

The access versus privacy trade-off is not one that pits law enforcement personnel wanting access against a citizenry wanting privacy. For one thing, the Freedom of Information Act at the federal level and its many state counterparts mandate some degree of open access to public information.[2] Public opinion supports freedom of information. One survey found that "most [people] are willing to give up some privacy protection if the trade-off results in a benefit to the public, such as increased safety, crime prevention, or the protection of children" (Ellard 2000).

A key part of the new emphasis on community policing is information sharing about crime trends with community groups, and crime maps have been found to be a very popular tool for conveying complex crime-related data. Citizens may want crime-related data to make decisions on home protection, where to go to school, where and when to shop, and other basic life choices. Citizens want this information and often feel they have a right to it, and when government agencies offer crime data, there is a demand for it. For instance, the U.S. Department of Education has a popular website (http://ope.ed.gov/security) offering crime data on all colleges and universities, which parents and students may use as one criterion in selecting which colleges to attend. Likewise, the city of Milwaukee offers a comprehensive website with access not only to crime information but also data on tax parcel ownership, property violations, and even garbage routes.[3]

At the same time, the U.S. Constitution guarantees certain privacy rights, including rights applying to criminals. The principle of presumption of innocence before being found guilty forbids divulging information on suspects. It is not only criminals and suspects who want privacy, however. Victims of crime very often want privacy too, fearing re-victimization by a criminal or their associates. Release of a crime map showing the location of sexual assaults might pinpoint the addresses of sexual assault victims, for instance, violating their privacy. At the same time, failure to release such a map may prevent community residents from learning about critical dangers of which they have a right to be aware. Crime mappers must balance such conflicting demands by adopting a strategy that provides the community with enough information but does not violate the privacy of specific individuals. For instance, a crime map might display sexual assault locations to the nearest 100-block address rather than to actual residential addresses, thereby providing community warning information without identifying individual victims. However, such a strategy means that the original crime database with actual residential addresses must be protected from general access.

There is also an issue of liability of law enforcement agencies with respect to the release of false information. For instance, police departments have published incorrect addresses of released sex offenders under Megan's Law and opened themselves to the threat of lawsuits. Liability for false information is another reason in addition to safeguarding privacy that law enforcement agencies wish not to release information that pinpoints individuals.

To take another example, it is in the interest of law enforcement agencies and the citizenry alike that trends in crime be understood. Toward that end, researchers and analysts commonly want access to geocoded crime data. Often the potential for privacy violation by researchers is handled by requiring researchers to sign confidentiality agreements regarding release of data in research publications. Unfortunately, in practice law enforcement agencies may not yet have standardized such confidentiality requirements, or, if they have, they may not devote resources to assuring compliance.

To cope with the legal issues of providing data over the Internet, many law enforcement agencies require the user to electronically accept a disclaimer before accessing crime data or maps. Disclaimers are used to minimize agencies' liability from the improper use of both data and maps (Wartell and McEwen 2001). Just like confidentiality statements, disclaimers have no standardized format. Wartell and McEwen (2001) suggest, at a minimum, that departments using disclaimers first establish from what liability the department is seeking release. For example, does a department seek release from providing the data or from interpretations of the data as well as the map? Recall that one of the strengths of a GIS is the ability to draw new relationships from existing data. Other possible information to include is the geocoding or "hit" rate as well as a sample explanation of what these numbers might indicate to the data consumer.

Data privacy and confidentiality are concerns of citizens in a marketplace of instant information through electronic databases. Law enforcement agencies are mandated by various laws and procedures to collect a variety of information, some of it personal, that becomes public record accessible by fellow citizens. At the same time, police agencies seek to reasonably protect the victims of crimes from an unwarranted intrusion of their privacy. Even if they are not perfect, when they are used together confidentiality statements and data disclaimers are tools to reassure citizens that consideration is being given to privacy concerns by law enforcement agencies (Wartell and McEwen 2001).

Social Policy Issues
and Crime Mapping Data

A broader issue of data privacy has to do with social policy implications of releasing crime data, even when the privacy of specific individuals is not affected. It is entirely possible, for example, that the release of data on community crime patterns might be used by financial institutions to implement the illegal practice of "redlining," denying home loans or insurance to residents and business owners in high-crime neighborhoods. This particular scenario could be a reality if a choropleth map was to indicate the amount of crime located within a boundary area rather than more specifically where the crime was located.

On the other hand, releasing crime information can have the opposite effect. One researcher found only small portions of a neighborhood were affected by gang activity (Tita 1999). The sharing of maps highlighting this fact would discourage the flight of ordinary citizens and encourage continued business investment in the area. Additionally, by indicating where the crime is located and sharing that information, the police department may be able to use a community approach to address the problem and essentially reverse the "broken windows" theory of how crime spreads in this instance.

Because the release of crime information can have effects that cut both ways, law enforcement agencies rarely suppress crime information for broad social policy reasons. Moreover, many take the view of Professor James Meeker (UC-Irvine), who writes, "Since the law places no limits on what may be done with public information, it follows that law enforcement agencies are not responsible for misuse of public information that they are required by law to release" (Meeker 1999). Although it is possible to establish systems of firewalls, password protection, encryption, and other information security measures, law enforcement agencies fear there is no foolproof method of assuring that data will not fall into the wrong hands or, for that matter, be abused by law enforcement employees themselves.

There are also, of course, dangers and liabilities associated with dissemination of crime data. Data may reveal to criminals which neighborhoods are less targeted for police resources. During a lecture on GIS capabilities to law enforcement officials by one of the authors, a sheriff's deputy noted that if crime and arrest data were displayed on the Web, then criminals could determine the patrolling patterns used by the department. Despite this possibility, no cases of criminal counterintelligence using GIS crime maps have been reported. In terms of dissemination, the law enforcement community is still in the early stages of providing information through the Internet. So it is possible that future criminals may develop the sophistication to plan crimes based on public information. For example, by noting the concentration of crimes in a certain area of a police sector, one might guess that the police are focusing their patrol efforts in that location. A potential criminal may gamble on an easier opportunity to commit crimes where the police are not patrolling.

Data may be used by commercial firms (e.g., security agencies) to contact citizens intrusively by targeting residents based on crime areas. Resistance to Internet distribution of community crime data may arise from real estate interests and even homeowners concerned with the effect of such information on property values or the possibility of attracting further crime. Often this resistance is contrasted with use by people who are relocating to unfamiliar areas of the country. Some police agencies began providing crime maps on the Internet as a time-saving response to satisfying the routine requests for crime data from potential homebuyers.

In many ways the social policy issues of computerized crime mapping are interlaced with ethical decisions made in the light of using new technology. Onsrud (1995) notes that there is a gray area in using GIS technologies where decisions are technically legal and yet simultaneously unethical.

The ability to create new information from existing data contributes to this gray area. What is legal is often easier to understand than what is considered ethical behavior. After all, possessing and collecting certain types of data are not illegal as governments at all levels are prolific collectors and users. For example, as part of a community policing program, where is the line between proactive analysis of a community's needs and intrusive surveillance? The difference may be an ethical rather than legal distinction.

In the field of crime mapping, the Massachusetts Association of Crime Analysts in its *Crime Analyst's Bible* devotes a section of the handbook to ethics in crime analysis. On its website there is also a set of guidelines called "The Ten Commandments of Crime Analysis" at http://www.macrimeanalysts.com/tencom.html. The "commandments" are a general professional guide that author Christopher Bruce developed to help define what a crime analyst does and should be doing. As GIS technologies have progressed, the field has also engaged in self-examination of what constitutes the good and bad use of GIS. The Urban Regional Information Systems Association publishes a website of that association's ethical guide as well as an online bibliography of other ethical topics at http://www.urisa.org/ethics/code_of_ethics.htm.

Summary

Computerized crime mapping gives law enforcement agencies the capability to create new relationships from existing data. Along with this capability are concerns for personal privacy. In the past, police records existed in paper files with a time lag before a significant amount of data could be assembled into information. Now, by using the database component of a GIS, available data may be searched, matched, and even displayed on the Internet almost instantaneously. Due to the ease of creating and displaying information, a new sensitivity has been developing among crime analysts regarding the protection of victim identities and addresses.

In addition to the issues of personal privacy, there are also social policy issues associated with computerized crime mapping. Again, many of these issues are generated by the ability to create and instantly display data in new relationships to each other. An example of such a social policy issue is that of depressing real estate values and "redlining" neighborhoods where crime maps show them as excessively dangerous. Initially crime maps were offered to the public without comment to allow citizens to draw their own conclusions about the data. More recently, the trend is to provide enough commentary to explain concepts like geocoding rates and crime density.

Questions

1. Identify some reasons why citizens would want easy access to crime data.
2. What are some reasons for maintaining the confidentiality of certain crime information?
3. What are some legal tools used by police departments to lessen liability exposure for providing crime data over the Internet?
4. From a social policy standpoint, what is one hazard of using choropleth maps?
5. What are some possible ways a criminal could use Internet crime data?
6. How could using crime-mapping data be legal yet not ethical?

CHAPTER 8

Conclusion

Crime Mapping Today

The field of computerized crime mapping is comparatively young, and for many years only a few large police departments had the resources to use this technology. As computers became less costly, more compact, and increasingly powerful, GIS software followed the migration to desktop and network computing. This trend helped to place computerized crime mapping within the reach of even more and even smaller departments. Because these developments are so recent, few studies provide any information on how the technology is employed.

To determine the spread of computerized crime mapping, the Crime Mapping Research Center surveyed a national sample of police and sheriffs' departments. The survey was conducted in a 15-month period beginning in March 1997 and ending in May 1998. Demographically, the departments were classified as either large or small regardless of the community population they were serving. A department was considered large if there were more than 100 sworn officers and small if there were fewer (Mamalian and LaVigne 1999).

The survey results indicated that 13% of the sampled departments were then using computerized crime mapping. Although powerful computers and sophisticated software are more widely available, the larger departments continued to dominate in using computerized crime mapping. Larger police departments constituted 36% of the users in the sample as opposed to smaller departments, who were 3% of the users. The survey also highlighted the relative youth of computerized crime mapping among the responding departments. The average length of time departments reported using computerized crime mapping was 3.3 years (Mamalian and LaVigne 1999).

Diffusion of Computerized Crime Mapping

In delivering the keynote address at the fifth Annual Crime Mapping Conference in 2001, police scholar David Weisburd noted that the use of computerized crime mapping has been accelerating among departments for the past few years, especially since 1996. Basing his observations on a pilot study he conducted with colleagues at the University of Maryland, Weisburd also noted that computerized crime mapping appears to be following a recognizable "innovation curve" as it diffuses among police departments. In terms of the innovation curve, the diffusion of computerized crime mapping among police departments appears to be between one-half and two-thirds complete (Weisburd and Lum 2001).

Crime mapping today is an integral part of larger police departments and an important tool in combating crime. The results of both the CMRC survey and Weisburd and Lum's pilot study indicate the field of computerized crime mapping has the potential to grow for the next few years, especially in the medium-to-small jurisdictions. As part of the University of Maryland pilot study, Weisburd and Lum (2001) asked departments why they began to use computerized crime mapping. The most frequent answer was that departments started using crime mapping to facilitate hotspot policing, which was part of the paradigm shift moving the law enforcement community from reactive to proactive policing (Weisburd and Lum 2001).

Recently the emphasis on homeland security issues has further redirected some of the crime-mapping focus from hotspot analysis. Since one of the strengths of a GIS is creating new relationships from data, it is potentially an important tool for threat analysis. As part of doing threat analysis, analysts use some of the same skills developed in crime mapping to determine and prioritize the most likely terrorist targets (Helms 2002). The national interest in heightened security is one more force behind the recent expansion of crime mapping in law enforcement.

The Future of Crime Mapping

Computerized crime mapping has come a long way since the 1960s, when early crime maps were created at Harvard University using SYMAP software based on data input from punched cards (Eylon 2001). By the 1990s the advent of desktop computers had made crime maps accessible to even small law enforcement jurisdictions though user-friendly software like MapInfo and ArcView. Still, crime mapping is a relatively new tool for law enforcement. It was only in 1997 that the National Institute of Justice established the Crime Mapping Research Center to be a clearinghouse for the use of geographic information systems in law enforcement. Even today, access is not implementation, and, at the start of the new millennium, crime mapping remains largely a big city phenomenon with much progress remaining to be accomplished to exploit its full potential as a crime-fighting tool.

In the brief period since then, thousands of criminal justice agencies throughout the United States have incorporated GIS into their daily operations and have found new and creative uses for this important set of tools. The rapid evolution of this field calls for a peek at the future of crime mapping, a field destined to become an integral part of law enforcement strategic planning and daily operations management.

Harries (1999) inventoried several ways in which crime mapping will change in the future. Crime mapping will cease to be the province of large police departments, and urban-suburban-rural differences will diminish. Baseline maps will become standardized and readily available even for rural areas. GIS software will become more user-friendly, accessible, and inexpensive even as it incorporates more and more powerful methodologies. Cross-jurisdictional and regional approaches to crime mapping will become commonplace as data-sharing arrangements linking federal, state, and local agencies become institutionalized. Public access to crime data will increase, also making privacy protection a critical law enforcement management issue. And managerial evaluation and assessment of crime mapping itself will become commonplace as crime mapping emerges from its experimental stage (Boba 2000).

Integration with Legacy Databases

The coming decade will see the integration of "legacy" databases across city and country departments, creating uses and demands for crime maps by social workers, civic leaders, educators, recreation staff, and others far outside the traditional user base in police crime analysis units. The rise of wireless technology and real-time mapping will further expand the scope of uses for crime maps and enlarge the community of crime map users, many mobile computers in agency vehicles or even using palm-held computers in the field. San Diego Police Department information analyst Deena Bowman-Jamieson noted in this regard, "A new breed of GIS users within the law enforcement community are demanding greater access to GIS applications that support contingency planning, tactical planning and response, as well as innovative data visualization techniques and spatial models" (cited in Eylon 2001).

Integration with Other Technologies

The future of crime mapping also holds the closer integration of geographic information systems with other technologies. An illustration is ShotSpotter, a multi-technology innovation of the Redwood City, California, Police Department. ShotSpotter integrates GIS with real-time sound data collected from microphones in high-crime areas. Using mathematical software capable of triangulation, Redwood City police can detect gunshots in residential or business neighborhoods, displayed on a map for real-time response. Another example of technology integration is Dialogic Communications Corporation's "The Communicator" automated telephone notification system, used, for instance, by Overland Park (KS) Police Department to tie automated crime maps to automatic messages to citizens by telephone, pager, and fax regarding important crime bulletins (Tallman, Wernicke, and May 1999:12).

A far more pervasive illustration is that GIS packages in the future will become much more closely integrated with Global Positioning System technology. Global positioning units enable officers in the field to know their exact spatial position, information that currently is often collected for later download and input into GIS databases for mapping. As GIS packages are more integrated, however, it will become easier and easier to provide real-time updating of crime-mapping databases and downloading of real-time crime maps back to field officers (*Crime Mapping News* 1999b).

Integration with the Web

Leading GIS companies like ESRI (makers of ArcGIS) have ancillary products like ArcIMS and ArcIMS Route Server, which support dissemination of mapping services via the Internet, complete with end-user ability to display, query, and analyze local data instantly using their web browser. Sun

Microsystems, makers of Java, one of the leading programming languages for the web, has also launched GeoJava as a vehicle for distributed, web-based computing for spatial applications. GeoJava is already being used by the Bureau of the Census in a project to implement a spatially enabled data infrastructure. At a more general level, the emergence of Geography Markup Language (GML) brings to geographic information systems the power of XML, Extensible Markup Language. Geography markup language is a method to access geospatial databases. Java Location Services, from Sun, uses GML to implement maps for the web. Geography markup language also enables "Map Styles," allowing end-users to use their web browsers to make cutting-edge maps.

Mobility. In the future crime mapping will also become more mobile. It will be increasingly possible to obtain GIS analysis right in the field, in patrol cars, and even on handheld computers. GeoJava, though ObjectFX technology, is one of the stategies to implement GIS on portable personal digital assistants and software "appliances." Mobile GIS is a growing field in terms of hardware and software options. Some examples already available include ArcPad hand-held mapping software for the Windows CE environment for handhelds, using ArcView shapefiles compatible with the leading desktop mapping software from ESRI, Inc. Competitors include FieldWorker (using Oracle 8i Lite), GPSPilot.com (adds mapping to handheld Palm Pilots), StarPal (GIS software from HGIS, Inc., for Windows CE and other handheld systems), and Palm OS GIS Software (also for Palm Pilots and compatibles; others include MapFrame, PocketGIS, Solus, and Web-Mapper). Many of these systems function using wireless connections for true mobility in the field. MapXtend, for instance, uses MapInfo and Java technology to provide GIS functions for wireless personal digital assistants.

Miller (1987:312) pointed out that "mental imagery is a key ingredient in creative scientific thinking." The spatial imagery associated with mapping in law enforcement stimulates scientific investigation within the field of crime analysis. There are few other data visualization tools that can be used so effectively from the level of the beat cop to the highest levels of strategic decision-making in law enforcement. Equally useful in conveying crime trends and issues among detectives in team meetings, civil leaders in community policing, jurors in a legal setting, and elected officials in city council meetings, only the surface of the potential of crime mapping has been scratched. Crime mapping is a rapidly evolving tool for law enforcement, and it may be predicted safely that it will take its place as one of the most significant assets in the crime analyst's toolkit.

Summary

Thanks to the revolution in personal computers and software, crime mapping is spreading from large jurisdictions to smaller ones. The use of GIS technology in crime mapping is expected to continue growing. Based on the 1999 Crime Mapping Research Center Survey, 13% of the sampled departments were then using computerized crime mapping. Most departments began their computerized crime-mapping programs to identify the hotspots of crime as an aspect of community-oriented policing. Many crime-analysis software programs originally written by talented analysts are now available for purchase as off-the-shelf technology. This availability shortens the learning and application cycle for departments initiating their programs.

In the future, computerized crime mapping is expected to advance in two areas, mobility and integration. Robust communication systems and GIS software will provide crime maps to patrol officers while they are on the beat. Other options for the future include storing crime maps in personal digital assistants as part of the roll-call process. In the area of integration, there is a trend toward data sharing between police departments and other agencies. Access to new types of data will enable departments to continue their focus on proactive policing methods. Integration is also an emerging presence on police websites, as more interactive crime maps are made available to the public. Many of these maps feature other layers in addition to crime incidents and streets in order to display crime in its full social context. Crime mapping in the future will be even more central to law enforcement operations, from daily beat assignments to long-range strategic planning.

Questions

1. Overall, what percentage of police departments reported using computerized crime mapping?
2. Describe the distribution of police departments using computerized crime mapping.
3. At the time of the survey, what was the average length of time reported for using crime mapping?
4. What was the most frequent reason departments reported for initiating computerized crime mapping?
5. In the future, what are some possible uses of GIS in conjunction with global positioning systems (GPS)?
6. In the future, what two areas of computerized crime mapping are expected to advance significantly?

Law Enforcement Websites with Crime Maps

Many law enforcement agencies have moved their crime maps to the World Wide Web. Some of the agencies have an extensive and interactive presence while others display static maps and data. One of the advantages of a web presence is to provide an alternative means for citizens to make routine inquiries about criminal activity in their communities. Placing crime maps on the web is an efficient use of the analysts' as well as the citizen's time.

http://www.ojp.usdoj.gov/nij/maps/weblinks.html—The Mapping and Analysis for Public Safety Office maintains an extensive list of law enforcement websites that feature crime maps. Many of the departments have interactive crime maps as well as historical crime data.

http://www.portlandpolicebureau.com—The Portland Police Department operates an interactive crime-mapping site for the city called CrimeMapper. The application requires entering a street address before displaying the area of interest along with selected statistics.

http://baffle.pfeiffer.edu—The Charlotte-Mecklenburg (NC) Police Department's Reported Incidents Information System. Incident maps are available by discrete street address as well as intersection.

http://www.cityofchicago.org/CAPS—Chicago Police Department's Incident Collection for Automated Mapping. The Chicago online mapping includes incidents by address, police beat, intersecting streets, and by school.

http://samnet.isp.state.il.us/ispso2/samintro.htm—Illinois State Police, statewide mapping of crime incidents collected in the Illinois Uniform Crime Reports. The site uses choropleth mapping to display the density of crime.

http://www.jpso.com—The Jefferson Parish LA Sheriff 's Office provides crime mapping by zip code as well as yearly trends in selected crimes dating from 1999. The site is interactive.

http://www.ci.lincoln.ne.us/city/police—The Lincoln (NE) Police Department website is interactive, allowing the user to view a selection of crimes. The site also provides basic user education in the subject of interpreting crime maps as well as the process of geocoding addresses to create maps.

http://city.oakcc.com/maproom/crimewatch—The Oakland (CA) Police Department "Crimewatch" website allows the user to interactively map a selection of various crimes. The crimes are displayed by police beat and district as well as street address.

http://www.co.pierce.wa.us/abtus/ourorg/sheriff/—The Pierce

County (WA) Sheriff 's Office provides a sex offender registry with the capabilities to buffer an address and indicate the number of offenders living within a half-mile radius of the address.

http://pslgis.cityofpsl.com/—The City of Port St. Lucie, Florida, provides a daily update of crime incidents as well as crime statistics and interactive maps by police districts. The site also has a selection of static maps identifying the police districts and zones.

http:// www.sacpd.org/—The Sacramento (CA) Police Department interactive website permits database queries and display by neighborhood, intersection, and map selection. Additionally, the site displays the number and type of crime by buffering the selection at .25-mile intervals.

http://www.arjis.org—The Automated Regional Justice Information System (ARJIS) of San Diego County, California, provides crime maps of the communities within San Diego County participating in the ARJIS program. The ARJIS program is one of the few regional crime mapping and analysis programs in the country.

http://www.ci.scottsdale.az.us/police/CAU/Crime_data_by_beat. asp—The Scottsdale (AZ) Police Department has an interactive site that maps the location of crimes since January 1999. The site requires a brief detour to download AutoDesk's map viewer program before accessing any of the crime maps. Once you install the viewer it does not have to be downloaded again.

http://www.new_orleans.la.us/cnoweb/nopd/maps/basecrimemap .html—The City of New Orleans Police Department provides a weekly static display of crime maps for crimes committed in the city. There is also historical crime data for selected crimes dating from 1998.

http://www.evansvillepolice.com—The Evansville (IN) Police Department's website displays static weekly and monthly crime maps for the current year. The site also displays a monthly hotspot analysis for the city.

Notes

Chapter 1. Geographic Information Systems

1. For a similar example from the Cambridge (MA) Police Department see Bruce (2000).
2. This tutorial is available for download from the Crime Mapping Research Center's website at www.ojp.usdoj.gov/cmrc/training/welcome.html#crimemap. Users must have either ArcView GIS Version 3.x or MapInfo Professional 5.5 or higher. The tutorial author, Wilpin Gorr, also offers an expanded tutorial at http://www.heinz.cmu.edu/gistutorial.
3. These packages are available at http://www.usdoj.gov/criminal/gis/. The Regional Crime Analysis Geographic Information System is a crime-mapping, analysis, and reporting tool designed to promote a regional approach to crime mapping.

4. The web address is http://www.ojp.usdoj.gov/BJA/.
5. Police departments with crime mapping available via the Web include:

    Charlotte-Mecklenburg (NC) Police Department, http://cmpd.cicp.org,

    Chicago Police Department, http://www.cityofchicago.org/CAPS,

    Illinois State Police, http://samnet.isp.state.il.us/ispso2/samintro.htm,

    Jefferson Parish (LA) Sheriff 's Office, http://www.jpso.com,

    Lansing (MI) Police Department, http://www.lansingpolice.com,

    Lincoln (NE) Police Department, http://www.ci.lincoln.ne.us/city/police,

    Oakland (CA) Police Department, http://city.oakcc.com/maproom/crimewatch,

    Pierce County (WA) Sheriff 's Office, http://www.co.pierce.wa.us/abtus/ourorg/sheriff/,

    City of Port St.Lucie (FL), http://pslgis.cityofpsl.com,

    Sacramento (CA) Police Department, http:// www.sacpd.org,

    San Diego County (CA), http://www.arjis.org,

    Scottsdale (AZ) Police Department, http://www.ci.scottsdale.az.us/police/CAU/Crime_data_by_beat.asp.
6. The web address is http://samnet.isp.state.il.us/ispso2/samintro.htm.
7. The web address is http://www.ci. .cambridge.ma.us/ ∼ CPD/.
8. The web address is http://www.ci.austin.tx.us/police.
9. Geocoding is described in a law enforcement context in Crime Mapping Laboratory (2000b).
10. Information on interpreting geocoded data is found in the Police Foundation's publication, *Geocoding in Law Enforcement,* at the Office of Community Oriented Policing Services website at http://www.usdoj.gov/cops/pdf/cp_resources/e10990023.pdf.
11. A 2000 National Crime Mapping Research Center study of 28 jurisdictions providing crime maps on the Internet found only 7 included interpretations along with actual maps.
12. The Virginia site is at http://www.vsp.state.va.us.
13. The website address is http://www.co.pierce.wa.us/abtus/ourorg/sheriff/default.htm.

Chapter 2. Crime-Mapping Basics

1. Explanations of spatial statistics such as the Nearest-Neighbor Index or spatial autocorrelation may be found in introductory statistical geography textbooks.

2. Raster data is based a grid of cells covering an area of interest. The smallest unit of raster data within the grid is the pixel.

3. A spatial statistics program widely used by crime analysts is CrimeStat, available as free software from http://www.icpsr.umich.edu/NACJD/crimestat.html#SOFTWARE.

Chapter 3. Managing Crime with Spatial Tools

1. Remote sensing is a term generally applied to images collected actively or passively. The images may be collected by various electromagnetic or image gathering devices. For more information, see http://www.vtt.fi/tte/research/tte1/tte14/virtual/defin.html.

2. See National Institute of Justice/NCJRS study NCJ 191862, Demonstration of Orthophotographic Representation and Analysis. Final Research Report, Revised November 2001. Keith Harries, Principle Investigator

3. See the BJS site analysis of crime characteristics at http://www.ojp.usdoj.gov/bjs/

4. See Chapter 2 on mapping hotspots of crime.

5. See the MAPS website at http://www.ojp.usdoj.gov/nij/maps/tools.html for links to various crime analysis software packages.

6. More information about the census is available at http://www.census.gov

7. For more information regarding ArcView's redistricting extension, see ESRI's website at http://www.esri.com/software/arcview/extensions/district_extension.html.

8. More information about the MapInfo redistricting extension is available at http://www.mapinfo.com/industry/government/redistricting/index.cfm.

9. The statistics for the Baltimore County Police were taken from a posting on the CrimeMapping listserv. In later communications, author Wes Westerfield credits the efforts of Baltimore County Police Chief Statistician Phil Canter and staff with achieving notable savings of time using GIS technology.

Chapter 4. Modeling Crime with Spatial Tools

1. Source: http://www.ojp.usdoj.gov/cmrc/research/welcome.html #hotspot2. September 8, 2001. New Orleans, it may be noted, has an outstanding crime–mapping website allowing users to se-

lect a crime map by district, for various time periods: http://www. new_orleans.la.us/cnoweb/nopd/maps/basecrimemap.html.

2. More information about the census and the use of standard industry codes (SIC) is available at http:// www. Census.gov.

3. SPLANCS is an example of software for point-pattern analysis. See http://www.maths.lancs.ac.uk/ ~ rowlings/Splancs.html.

4. A VRML browser or plug-in such as CosmoPlayer is needed to view VRML maps.

5. For an example, see http://www.geovista.psu.edu/grants/dgp-99/feature.html. "Conditional Choropleth Maps: Dynamic Multivariate Representations of Statistical Data." Research conducted by Dan Carr, Alan MacEachren, Duncan McPherson, Erik Steiner, and Mark Hower.

Chapter 5. Crime Mapping and Police Decision-Making

1. More information about the SARA process is available at http:// www.usdoj.gov/cops/cp_resources/tools_tips/tt_sara.htm.

2. More information about the annual Herman Goldstein award may be found at http://www.policeforum.org/POPCall2002.txt.

3. Source: http://www.ojp.usdoj.gov/cmrc/research/welcome.html #bloodlead. September 8, 2001.

4. CrimePoint 2002 AutoTheft is software from Crime Prevention Analysis Lab, Inc., whose web address is http://www.crimepaterns.com/.

5. The *intranet* is a self-contained network inaccessible to outside users as opposed to the *Internet,* which allows connection between networks of users.

6. The State of Utah has posted a copy of a multi-agency MOU on its website at http://agrc.its.state.ut.us/gisac/mou.txt.

7. See the COMPASS websites for Seattle and Milwaukee at http:// www.ci.seattle.wa.us/planning/compass/faq.htm and http://www .milwaukee.gov/compass/.

Chapter 6. Crime Mapping for City Police Chiefs and County Sheriffs

1. The address is http://www.sacpd.org.

2. For another example, note the Evansville (IN) Police Department's website, located at http://www.evansvillepolice.com. The site features sector and police beat maps, crime charts and graphs,

weekly maps of location and frequency of crimes, and monthly maps of calls for service. Visitors can view selected complaints, crimes, and arrests.

3. There is a summary of this effort as well as contact information for the agency available on the Crime Mapping Research Center's website at http://www.ojp.usdoj.gov/cmrc/pubs/corrections.pdf.

4. For information on NYC's Compstat program, contact Assistant to the Chief of the Department, New York City Police Department, Suite 1300, 1 Police Plaza, New York, NY 10038; (212) 374-6710.

5. See the Philadelphia Police Department website at www.esri.com/industries/lawenforce/05_philapolice.html.

6. For more information, contact Police Commissioner, Philadelphia Police Department, One Franklin Square. Philadelphia, PA 19106; http://www.ppdonline.org/ppd_compstat.html/. CompStat Bulletin, a monthly newsletter, is also available.

Chapter 7. Public Concerns with Crime Mapping

1. This section is indebted to material drawn from this conference's report.

2. For further information on the Freedom of Information Act, see http://foia.fbi.gov.

3. The address is http:// www.gis.ci.mil.wi.us.

References

Alba, Richard, and John Logan (1992). Analyzing locational attainments: Constructing individual-level regression models using aggregate data. *Sociological Methods and Research*, 20 (3): 367–397.

Alexander, Monica, and Wei-Ning Xiang (1994). Crime pattern analysis using GIS. Urban and Regional Information Systems Association, *GIS/LIS* (1994): 1(3).

American City & County Staff (2000). Winston-Salem arrests juvenile crime with GIS. *American City & County* (November). Retrieved 4/10/02 from http://industryclick.com/magazinearticle.asp.

Anselin, Luc, Jacqueline Cohen, David Cook, Wilpen Gorr, and George Tita (2000). Spatial analysis of crime. In Duffee, David, ed. *Vol. 4. Measurement and Analysis of Crime and Justice*. 213–262 Washington, DC: U.S. Department of Justice.

Astor, R. A., H. A. Meyer, and W. Behre (1999). Unowned places and times: Maps and interviews about violence in high schools. *American Educational Research Journal* 36(1): 3–42.

Bair, Sean (2000). ATAC:A tool for tactical crime analysis. *Crime Mapping News* 2(2): 9–10

Barnes, G. C. (1995). Defining and optimizing displacement. In J.E. Eck and D. Weisburd, eds. *Crime and Place*. Monsey, NY: Criminal Justice Press; and Washington, DC: Police Executive Research Forum, pp. 95–113.

Bennett, Richard (1991). Development and crime: A cross-national, time-series analysis of competing models. *Sociological Quarterly* 32(3): 343–363.

Bibel, Dan (2000). Statewide crime analysis and mapping: An ongoing project. *Crime Mapping News* 2 (3): 1–4.

Blau, Judith, and Peter Blau (1982). The cost of inequality: Metropolitan structure and violent crime. *American Sociological Review* 47: 114–129.

Block, Carolyn Rebecca, Margaret Dabdoub, and Suzane Fregly (1995). *Crime Analysis Through Computer Mapping*. Washington, DC: Police Executive Research Forum.

Block, C. R. (1994). STAC hot spot areas: A statistical tool for law enforcement decisions. Proceedings of the Workshop on Crime Analysis Through Computer Mapping. Chicago: Illinois Criminal Justice Information Authority.

Block, Richard (1979). Community, environment, and violent crime. *Criminology* 17: 46–57.

Block, Richard, and Carolyn Block. (2000). The Bronx and Chicago. In *Analyzing Crime Patterns, Frontiers of Practice*. In Goldsmith, Victor, Phillip G. McGuire, John H. Mollenkopf, and Timothy A. Ross, eds. Thousand Oaks, CA: Sage Publications, Inc.

Boba, Rachel (1999). Using the Internet to disseminate crime information. *FBI Law Enforcement Bulletin* 68 (10): 6.

Boba, Rachel (2000). *Guidelines to Implement and Evaluate Crime Analysis and Mapping in Law Enforcement*. Washington, DC: Police Foundation. Report to the Office of Community Oriented Policing Services Cooperative Agreement #97-CK-WXK-004.

Boots, B.N., and A. Getis (1988). *Point Pattern Analysis*. Thousand Oaks, CA: Sage Publications.

Bowman-Jamieson, Deena, and Kurt Smith (2001). San Diego: Mapping schools and beyond. *Crime Mapping News* 3(2): 8–9.

Brantingham, Paul J., and Patricia L. Brantingham (1975). The spatial patterning of burglary. *Howard Journal of Penology and Crime Prevention* 14(2): 11–23.

Brantingham, Paul J., and Patricia L. Brantingham (1981). Notes on the geometry of crime. Pp. 27–54 in P.J. Brantingham and P.L. Brantingham, eds. *Environmental Criminology*. Beverly Hills, CA: Sage Publications.

Brantingham, Paul J., and Patricia L. Brantingham (1993). Nodes, paths and edges: Consideration on the complexity of crime and the physical environment. *Journal of Environmental Psychology* 13(1): 3–28.

Brassel, K. E., and J. J. Utano (1979). Linking crime and census information within a crime mapping system. *Review of Public Data Use* 7(3/4): 15–24.

Brown, M. A. (1982). Modeling the spatial distribution of suburban crime. *Economic Geography* 58(3): 247–261.

Brown, S., D. Lawless, X. Lu, and D.J. Rogers (1998). Interdicting a burglary pattern: GIS and crime analysis in the Aurora Police Department. Pp. 99–108 in N. La Vigne and J. Wartell, eds. *Crime Mapping Case Studies: Successes in the Field.* Washington, DC: Police Executive Research Forum.

Bruce, Chris (2000). Mapping in action-tactical crime analysis: Musings from the Cambridge, Massachusetts Police Department. *Crime Mapping News* 2(2): 10–12.

Buerger, Michael E., Ellen G. Cohn, and Anthony J. Petrosino (1995). "Defining the hot spots of crime": Operationalizing theoretical concepts for field research. In *Crime and Place.* Ronald V. Clark, ed. Monsey, NY: Criminal Justice Press.

Bureau of Justice Assistance (2001). An overview of OJP bureaus, offices and COPS information technology initiatives. Washington, DC: Bureau of Justice Assistance.

Burquest, R., G. Farrell, and K. Pease (1992). Lessons from schools. *Policing* 8(2): 148–155.

Bursik, Robert (1988). Social disorganization and theories of crime. *Criminology* 26:519–551.

Bursik, Robert, and Tim Webb (1982). Community change and patterns of delinquency. *American Journal of Sociology* (88): 24–42.

Butler, Boyd (2000). Mapping in action: Illinois methamphetamine risk-model. *Crime Mapping News* 2(4): 8–9.

Bynum, Timothy S. (2001) *Using Analysis For Problem Solving: A Guidebook for Law Enforcement.* Washington, DC: U.S. Department of Justice, Office of Community Oriented Policing.

Cadora, Eric, and Todd Clear (1999). Mapping for community justice programs. National Institute of Justice, Mapping in Corrections Resource Group Meeting, New York 22 August 1999.

Canter, P. (1995). State of the statistical art: Point-pattern analysis. In Block, Carolyn Rebecca, Margaret Dabdoub, and Suzane Fregly, eds. *Crime Analysis Through Computer Mapping* (pp. 151–160). Washington, DC: Police Executive Research Forum.

Carr, D., Wallin, J.F. and Carr, A. (2000). Two new templates for epidemiology applications: Linked micromap plots and conditioned choropleth maps. *Statistics in Medicine* 19: 2521–2538.

Casady, Tom (1999). Privacy issues in the presentation of geocoded data. *Crime Mapping News* 1(3): 1–3.

Caulkins, J., J. Cohen, and J. Wei (1996). Predicting criminal recidivism: A comparison of neural network models with statistical methods. *Journal of Criminal Justice* 24 (3).

Choldin, Harvey, and Dennis Roncek (1976). Density, population potential, and pathology: A block-level analysis. *Public Data Use* 4: 19–29.

Clarke, Keith C. (1997). *Getting Started with Geographic Information Systems*. Upper Saddle River, NJ: Prentice-Hall.

CMRC Staff (1998). *Crime Mapping Research Center Annual Report 1998*. Washington, DC: U.S. Department of Justice.

Coleman, Veronica, Holton, Walter C., Olson, Kristina, Robinson, Stephen C., Stewart, Judith (1999). Using knowledge and teamwork to reduce crime. *National Institute of Justice Journal* 241: 17–23.

Cooke, Thomas (1993). Proximity to job opportunities and African American male unemployment: A test of the spatial mismatch hypothesis in Indianapolis. *The Professional Geographer* 45: 407–415.

Corcoran, J., and J. A. Ware (2001). Data clustering using ANNs as a precursor to crime hot spot prediction. Dallas, TX: 2001 Crime Mapping Research Conference, U. S. Department of Justice.

Crime Mapping Laboratory (2000a). *Integrating Community Policing and Computer Mapping: Assessing Issues and Needs Among Cops Office Grantees*. Washington, DC: Police Foundation.

Crime Mapping Laboratory (2000b). *Geocoding in Law Enforcement*. Washington, DC: Police Foundation.

Crime Mapping Laboratory (2001). *Users' Guide to Mapping Software for Police Agencies*. Third edition. Washington, DC: Police Foundation.

Crime Mapping News (1999a). Technical discussion: An introduction to geocoding. *Crime Mapping News* 1(2): 3.

Crime Mapping News (1999b). Innovative mapping: GPS and GIS. *Crime Mapping News* 1(2):6.

Crime Mapping Research Center (2001). *Why Map Crime? CMRC Briefing Book*. Retrieved 11/2/2001 from http://www.ojp.usdoj.gov/cmrc/briefingbook/welcome.html.

Crime Mapping Research Center (2002). *Funding opportunities*. Retrieved 11/2/2001 from http:// www.ojp.usdoj.gov/cmrc/funding/welcome.html.

Department of Justice (2002). U.S. Department of Justice (USDOJ). Retrieved January 21, 2002 from http://www.usdoj.gov/.

Deutsch, J. (1984). Interjurisdictional criminal mobility: A theoretical perspective. *Urban Studies* (21): 451–458.

Eck, John E. (1995). Drug markets and drug places: A case-control study of the spatial structure of illicit drug dealing. *Dissertation Abstracts International, The Humanities and Social Sciences,* 56 (1).

Eck, John E. (2002). Crossing the borders of crime: Factors influencing the utility and practicality of interjurisdictional crime mapping. *Human and Technological Barriers in Crime Mapping* (1), 1–16. Washington, DC: Police Foundation.

Eck, John E., and W. Spelman (1988). *Problem Solving: Problem-Oriented Policing in Newport News.* Washington, DC: Police Executive Research Forum.

Eck, John E., and William Spelman (2002). Who ya gonna call? the police as problem busters. *Crime and Delinquency* 33(1): 31–52.

Elber, Gail (2001). Taking a bite out of crime mapping: Making push-pins obsolete. *Geospatial Solutions* 11(5): 19–20.

Elie, Daniel (1994). Spatial analysis of crime. *Criminologie,* 27(1): 7–21.

Elie, Daniel, and Pierre Legendre (1992). Spatial autocorrelation and the displacement of criminality. *Criminologie* 25 (2): 139–154.

Ellard, Timothy (2000). Public attitudes toward uses of criminal history information. SEARCH National Conference on Privacy, Technology, and CJ Information, May 31, 2000. Source: http://www.search.org/conferences/priv_tech_2000/Agenda.htm, June 15, 2000.

Elliot, Martin, and Jerry Wagner (2000). School hostage drill demonstrates importance of mapping technology. *Police Chief* 67 (9): 50–55.

Eylon, Lili (2001). GIS-a powerful weapon in the fight against crime. *GIS Vision.* (August). Retrieved 11/12/2001 from http://www.gisvisionmag.com/Feature/crime1.php.

Feliciano, Bob (2001). Mapping our schools makes sense: Creating a tactical plan for school violence using GIS. *Crime Mapping News* 3(2):1–4.

Felson, M. (1987). Routine activities and crime prevention in the developing metropolis. *Criminology* 24(4): 911–931.

Fyfe, Nicholas (1991). The police, space, and society: The geography of policing. *Progress in Human Geography* 5(3): 249–267.

Garson, G. David (1998). *Neural Networks: An Introductory Guide for Social Scientists.* London: Sage Publications.

Garson, G. David, and Robert S. Biggs (1992). *Analytic Mapping and Geographic Databases.* Newbury Park, CA: Sage Publications.

Garson, G. David, and Irvin B. Vann (2001). *Geographic Information Systems for Small and Medium Law Enforcement Jurisdictions: Strategies and Effective Practices.* Raleigh, NC: Governor's Crime Commission.

Geake, Elisabeth (1993). How PC's predict where crime will strike. *New Scientist* 140: 17.

Geggie, P.F. (1998). Mapping and serial crime prediction. Pp. 109–116 in N. La Vigne and J. Wartell, eds., *Crime Mapping Case Studies: Successes in the Field*. Washington, DC: Police Executive Research Forum.

Giuliani, Rudolph W. (1997). Innovative computer mapping program has reduced crime to its lowest levels in 30 years. Keynote address at International COMPSTAT Conference. Retrieved on 04/16/02 from http://www.ci.nyc.ny.us/html/om/html/97/sp268–97.html.

Goldstein, Herman (1979). Improving policing: A problem-oriented approach. *Crime and Delinquency* 25:236–258.

Goldstein, Herman (1990). *Problem Oriented Policing*. New York: McGraw-Hill.

Gottfredson, Denise (1991). Social area influences on delinquency: Multilevel analysis. *Journal of Research in Crime and Delinquency* 28: 197–226.

Greenwald, Michael J. (2000). Beyond city limits: The multi-jurisdictional applications of GIS. *Journal of the Urban and Regional Information Systems Association* 12(1): 31–43.

Groff, Elizabeth R., and Nancy G. LaVigne (1998). The use of geographic information systems (GIS) for state and local crime analysis. Paper presented at Conference of European Statisticians, October 5–7, 1998.

Hakim, Simon, and Andrew Buck (1989). Do casinos enhance crime? *Journal of Criminal Justice* 17(5): 409–416.

Hammitt, Harry (2000). Personal issues: Courts wrestle with what to post. *Government Technology* 13 (4): 62.

Harries, Keith (1999). *Mapping Crime: Principle and Practice*. Washington, DC: Crime Mapping Research Center, National Institute of Justice. Retrieved from on 11/11/01 http://www.ncjrs.org/html/nij/mapping/.

Harries, Keith (2001). Demonstration of orthophotographic representation and analysis. Final research report, revised November 2001. NCJ 191862. Rockville, MD: National Institute of Justice/NCJRS.

Harris, Richard (1999). Mapping for state corrections. National Institute of Justice, Mapping in Corrections Resource Group Meeting. New York, 22 August 1999.

Hartman, Donna (2001). Crimemap: 2238. Communication to Crime-Map listserv, crimemap@lists.aspensys.com, 9/20/01.

Helms, Dan (2000). Trendspotting: Serial crime detection with GIS. *Crime Mapping News* 2(2): 5–8.

Helms, Dan (2002). Closing the barn door: Police counterterrorism after 9–11 from the analyst's perspective. *Crime Mapping News* 4 (1): 1–5. Washington, DC: Police Foundation, Crime Mapping Laboratory.

HIDTA (2001). Washington/Baltimore high intensity drug trafficking area mapping. Washington, DC: W/B HIDTA. Obtained 11/11/01 from http://www.hidta.org/services/mapping.asp.

Howard, Jim (2002). Incident level GIS. *Crime Mapping News* 4(1): 6–8.

Hubbs, R. (1998). The Greenway rapist case: Matching repeat offenders with crime locations. Pp. 93–98 in N. LaVigne and J. Wartell, eds., *Crime Mapping Case Studies: Successes in the Field*. Washington, DC: Police Executive Research Forum.

Hyatt, Robert A. (1999). Guidebook for measuring crime in public housing with geographic information systems. Washington, DC: U.S. Department of Housing and Urban Development.

Jackson, Pamela (1984). Opportunity and crime: A function of city size. *Sociological and Social Science Research* 68: 172–193.

Jefferis, Eric (1998). A multi-method exploration of crime hot spots; introduction. Presented at 1998 Academy of Justice Sciences (ACJS) Annual Conference. Washington, DC.

Johnson, Al (2001). The Austin Police Department's Crime Mapping Viewer. *Crime Mapping News* 3(3): 5–6.

Johnson, Melissa (2000). Applying theory to crime mapping. *Crime Mapping News* 2 (4):5–7.

Juppenlatz, Morris, and Xiaofeng Tian. (1996). *Geographic Information Systems and Remote Sensing*. Sydney: McGraw-Hill.

Kelly, Joe (1999). MapInfo-helps to take a byte out of crime. *Crime Mapping News* 1(4): 5–7.

Kern, Gary M. (1989). A computer simulation model for the study of police patrol deployment. *Simulation*. 52(6): 226–232.

Landsbergen Jr., David, and George Walken Jr. (2001). Realizing the promise: Government information systems and the fourth generation of information technology. *Public Administration Review* 61 (2): 206–220.

LaVigne, Nancy (1999). Computerized mapping as a tool for problem-oriented policing. *Crime Mapping News* 1(1): 1–3.

LaVigne, Nancy, and Julie Wartell (2000), *Mapping Crime Case Studies. Successes in the Field, Volume 2*. Washington, DC: Police Forum.

LaVigne, Nancy, and Julie Wartell (2001). *Mapping Across Boundaries*. Washington, DC: Police Executive Research Foundation.

LeBeau, James (1992). Four case studies illustrating the spatial-temporal analysis of serial rapists. *Police Studies* 15(3): 124–145.

LeBeau, James (1997). *Mapping Violence and High-Frequency Calls for Police Services*. Final Report. National Institute of Justice Award No. 94–IJ-CX-0045.

Levine, Ned (1999). CrimeStat: A spatial statistics program for the analysis of crime incident locations. Annandale, VA & Washington, DC: Ned Levine and Associates and the National Institute of Justice.

Ley, D., and R. Cybriwsky (1974). The spatial ecology of stripped cars. *Environment and Behavior*, 6: 53–68.

Lodha, Suresh K., and Arvind Verma (1999). Animations of crime maps using virtual reality modeling language. *Western Criminology Review* 1 (2). [Online]. Available: http://wcr.sonoma.edu/v1n2/lodha.html.

MacAlister, Bruce R. (1996). Local government city police share GIS. *GIS World* 9(4).

Mamalian, Cynthia A., and Nancy G. LaVigne (1999). The use of computerized crime mapping by law enforcement: Survey results. *National Institute of Justice Research Preview.* Available: http://www.ncjrs.org/pdffiles1/fs000237.pdf

Maltz, Michael D., Andrew C. Gordon, and Warren Friedman (1991). *Mapping Crime in Its Community Setting: Event Geography Analysis.* New York: Springer-Verlag.

McKay, Jim (2001). Ending the pawnshop paper trail. *Government Technology,* 14(10): 38.

Meeker, James (1999). Accountability for inappropriate use of crime maps and the sharing of inaccurate data. Part of "Crime mapping and data confidentiality roundtable notes," Washington, DC: Crime Mapping Research Center. Available on the web at http://www.ojp.usdoj.gov/cmrc/pubs/privacy/meeker.pdf.

Miller, Arthur I. (1987). *Imagery in Scientific Thought.* Cambridge, MA: MIT Press.

Mitchell, Andy (1999). *The ESRI Guide to GIS Analysis.* Redlands, CA: Environmental Systems Research Institute.

Mixdorf, Wayne (1999). Mapping for probation and parole. National Institute of Justice, Mapping in Corrections Resource Group Meeting, New York, 22 August 1999.

Morenoff, Jeffrey D., Robert J. Sampson, and Stephen W. Raudenbush (2001). *Neighborhood Inequality, Collective Efficacy, and the Spatial Dynamics Of Urban Violence.* Ann Arbor: Population Studies Center, Institute for Social Research, University of Michigan. Research Report No. 00–451 (revised, March 2001).

Mumm, A. J. (2001). Sounding the alarm on tornado sirens. *Geospatial Solutions* 11(5): 22.

National Institute of Justice. (n.d). *About NIJ.* Retrieved November 22, 2002, from http://www.ojp.usdoj.gov/nij/about.htm

National Law Enforcement and Corrections Technology Center (NLECTC) (2001). *A Guide for Applying Information Technology in Law Enforcement.* Maura Maness, ed. Rockville, MD: National Law Enforcement and Corrections Technology Center.

National Partnership for Reinventing Government (1999). Mapping Out Crime: *Report of the Task Force on Crime Mapping and Data Driven Management.* Washington, DC: U.S. Department of Justice.

Norton, Nat (2001). CrimeMap: 2257. Communication to CrimeMap listserv, crimemap@lists.aspensys.com, 9/26/01.

Office of Community Oriented Policing (2001). *SARA Model Approach to Problem Solving.* Washington, DC: U.S. Department of Justice.

O'Kane, James, R. Fisher, and Lorraine Green (1994). Mapping campus crime. *Security Journal* 5(3):172–180.

Olligschlaeger, A.M. (1997). Artificial neural networks and crime mapping. Pp. 313–347 in D. Weisburd and J. T. McEwen, eds. *Crime Mapping and Crime Prevention.* Monsey, NY: Criminal Justice Press.

Onsrud, H.J. (1995). Identifying unethical conduct in the use of GIS. *Cartography and Geographical Information Systems* 22, 90–97.

Openshaw, S., D. Waugh, A. Cross, C. Brunsdon, and J. Lillie (1991). Crime pattern analysis system for subdivisional use. *Police Requirements Support Unit Bulletin.* 41.

Osborne, Deborah (2001). "Re: Bryan's question." Communication to CrimeMap listserv, crimemap@lists.aspensys.com, 9/7/2001.

Paul, Bryant (2001). Using crime mapping to measure the negative secondary effects of adult businesses in Fort Wayne, Indiana: A quasi-experimental methodology. Paper presented to National Institute of Justice, Crime Mapping Research Center, 2001 International Crime Mapping Research Conference: Dallas, TX.

Paulson, Derek J. (2001). Mapping in podunk: Issues and problems in the implementation and use of GIS in small and rural law enforcement agencies. Paper presented to National Institute of Justice, Crime Mapping Research Center, 2001 International Crime Mapping Research Conference: Dallas, TX.

Police Executive Research Forum (2002). About the Herman Goldstein award. Available on the web at http://www.policeforum.org/POP Call2002.txt.

Ratcliffe, J. H., and M. J. McCullagh (1998). Identifying repeat victimization with GIS. *British Journal of Criminology* 38 (4): 651–662.

Ratcliffe, J. H., and M. J. McCullagh (1999). Burglary, victimisation and social deprivation. *Crime Prevention and Community Safety: An International Journal* 1(2): 37– 46.

Reporters Committee for Freedom of the Press (1998). Exemptions and privacy concerns. Retrieved online at http://www.rcfp.org/elecrecs/er_privacyconcerns.html on 4/10/02.

Rich, Thomas F. (1995). The use of computerized mapping in crime control and prevention programs. *NIJ Research in Action.* Retrieved online at http://www.nlectc.org/pdffiles/riamap.pdf.

Rich, Thomas (1999). Mapping the path to problem solving. *National Institute of Justice Journal.* 241: 1–8. Available on line at http://www.ojp.usdoj.gov/nij/journals/jr000241.htm.

Rich, Thomas F. (2001). *School COP:* Software for analyzing and mapping school incidents. *Crime Mapping News* 3 (2): 4.

Rocheleau, Bruce (1995). Computers and horizontal information sharing in the public sector. In Onsrud, Harlan J and Gerald Rushton,
eds. *Sharing Geographic Information Systems.* New Brunswick, NJ:
Center for Urban Policy Research.

Rogerson, P., and Y. Sun (2001). Spatial monitoring of geographic patterns: An application to crime analysis. *Computers, Environment
and Urban Systems,* 25: 539–556.

Rohe, William M. (2001). Community policing and planning. *Journal
of the American Planning Association* 67 (1): 78–98.

Roncek, D.W., and R. Bell (1981). Bars, blocks, and crimes. *Journal of
Environmental Systems,* 11: 35–47.

Rossmo, D. Kim (1995). Place, space, and police investigations: Hunt-
ing serial violent criminals. In J.E. Eck and D. Weisburd, eds.,
Crime and Place, *Crime Prevention Studies, Vol. 4.* Monsey, NY:
Criminal Justice Press.

Rossmo, D. Kim, and Anne Davies (2001). Stealth predator patterns.
Crime Mapping News 3(4): 6–7.

Scott, Michael S. (2000). Problem Oriented Policing: Reflections on
the First 20 Years. Washington, DC: U.S. Department of Justice, Office of Community Oriented Policing Services.

Schulman, Beth (2001). CrimeView Internet at the Redlands Police
Department. *Crime Mapping News* 3(4): 8–9.

SEARCH, The National Consortium for Justice Information and Statistics (2001). Integration in the context of justice information systems:
a common understanding. Sacramento, CA: SEARCH The National
Consortium for Justice Information and Statistics. Available online at
http://www.search.org/integration/pdf/Integration%20def.pdf.

Shaw, C., and H. McKay (1942). *Juvenile Delinquency and Urban Areas.*
Chicago: Chicago University Press.

Sherman, Lawrence R., Patrick R Gartin, and Michael E. Buerger.
1989. Hot spots of predatory crime: Routine activities and the
criminology of place. *Criminology* 17: 27–55.

Smith, Kurt (2001). Mapping narcotics activity information: Linking
patrol and investigations. *Crime Mapping News* 3(4): 4–5.

Stull, Judith C. (1994). Convict: A computer simulation of the criminal
justice system. *Computers in Human Services* 11(3/4): 261–268.

Sweeney, Wayne (2001). CrimeMap: 2255. Communication to Crime-
Map listserv, crimemap@lists.aspensys.com, 9/26/01.

Tallman, Gerald G., Susan Wernicke, and Jamie May (1999). Mapping
in action: Overland Park Police Department. *Crime Mapping News*
1(4):10—12.

Theodore, Jesse (2001). Crime mapping goes Hollywood: CBS 's The
District demonstrates crime mapping to millions of TV viewers.
Crime Mapping News 3(3): 7–10.

Thill. Jean-Claude, and Zongxiang Yang (1999). Detection of hot spots in geo-spatial databases. Online report, http://www.geog.buffalo.edu/ucgis/thill_proj.html, retrieved 4/10/02.

Thomas, Lt. Ricky (1999). Free maps to Drug Law Enforcement Agencies from the National Guard. *Crime Mapping News* 1(2): 1–2.

Tita, George (1999). Communication to CrimeMap listserv, crimemap@lists.aspensys.com, 1/12/99.

Vann, Irvin B., and Johnathon Lewin (2000). Personal Communication between Irvin Vann and Johnathon Lewin.

Velasco, Mary, and Rachael Boba (2000a). Tactical crime analysis and geographic information systems: Concepts and examples. *Crime Mapping News* 2 (2) 2. Washington, DC: Police Foundation.

Velasco, Mary, and Rachel Boba (2000b). *Manual of Crime Analysis Map Production*. Washington, DC: Police Foundation. Report to the Office of Community Oriented Policing Services Cooperative Agreement #97-CK-WXK-004.

Walcott, Susan M. (2000). Burglary. In *Atlas of Crime: Mapping the Criminal Landscape*.Turnbull Linda S., Elaine Hallisey Hendrix, et al., eds. Phoenix, AZ: Oryx Press.

Wartell, Julie (2001). Evaluating a crime mapping website. *Crime Mapping News* 3(3):1–4.

Wartell, Julie, and J. Thomas McEwen (2001). *Privacy in the Information Age: A Guide For Sharing Crime Maps and Spatial Data Series*. Washington, DC: National Institute of Justice. Available online at http://www.ncjrs.org/txtfiles1/nij/188739.txt.

Weisburd, David, and L. Green (1995). Measuring immediate spatial displacement: Methodological issues and problems. In J.E. Eck and D. Weisburd, eds. *Crime and Place*. Monsey, NY: Criminal Justice Press; and Washington, DC: Police Executive Research Forum, pp. 349–361.

Weisburd, David, and Cynthia Lum (2001). Translating research into practice: Reflections on the diffusion of crime mapping innovation. Keynote address presented to National Institute of Justice, Crime Mapping Research Center 2001 International Crime Mapping Research Conference Dallas, TX.

Weisburd, David, and Tom McEwan, eds. (1997). *Crime mapping and Crime Prevention*. Monsey, NY: Criminal Justice Press.

GENERAL EDITORS
David A. Schultz & Christina DeJong

Studies in Crime and Punishment is a multidisciplinary series that publishes scholarly and teaching materials from a wide range of methodological perspectives and explores sentencing and criminology issues from a single nation or comparative perspective. Subject areas to be addressed in this series include, but will not be limited to: criminology, sentencing and incarceration, policing, law and the courts, juvenile crime, alternative sentencing methods, and criminological research methods.

For additional information about this series or for the submission of manuscripts, please contact:

David A. Schultz
Peter Lang Publishing
Acquisitions Department
275 Seventh Avenue, 28th floor
New York, New York 10001

To order other books in this series, please contact our Customer Service Department:

(800) 770-LANG (within the U.S.)
(212) 647-7706 (outside the U.S.)
(212) 647-7707 FAX

Or browse online by series:
www.peterlangusa.com